# ADHD
# ORGANIZATION
# AND CLEANING

Simple Solutions To Quickly Get Organized,
Stay Organized Long Term, and Make
Cleaning With ADHD Easier

## Calvin Caufield

# Table of Contents

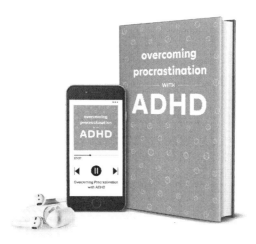

Get your Audiobook and eBook:

# Overcoming Procrastination with ADHD:
## Ditch Toxic Productivity & Use Neurodivergent Strategies That Actually Help

There's a lot of advice out there on how to deal with procrastination. You've probably heard a lot of it. But there's always one piece of crucial information left out in this advice – that it was designed for neurotypical people.

This audiobook will help you learn neurodivergent friendly techniques to start overcoming procrastination today.

*To get your copy scan the QR code below.*

# Part 1

## Making Organization and Cleaning Easy – Even With ADHD

# Introduction

Growing up, I always kept my bedroom door shut. If people came over, I imagined them asking, "How can you live like that?" I was embarrassed.

I didn't want to draw the looks or comments from my parents, who had long given up on telling me to clean my room.

I took my first crack at home organization when I was 6. "Clean your room," they said. "We want everything off the floor."

I was proud of my out-of-the-box thinking when I announced I was done.

"It's just a blanket on the floor. I like it there." It certainly looked like an improvement to me.

No toys or clothes were in sight, but that blanket was pretty lumpy.

That's part of it for us, though. Out of sight, out of mind. Because if there is too much in sight, we have no idea where to start, mental overload, and we go find something else to work on.

I wouldn't recognize that I had ADHD for another 20 years. Despite the books and papers embarrassingly falling out of my school locker every time I opened it, constantly forgetting things I needed, teachers calling home because I was 'zoning out' in class, and setting the kitchen toaster on fire twice - we only got the pop-up ones after that. The ones that stayed on until you decided your food was done were a hazard in our house. I'd forget I had food in there at all.

These were just deemed character flaws. That's just the way he is. That kind of thinking had me trying all of the typical suggestions. Just put it back when you're done using it. Make yourself a list. Clean your room once a day, and then you can keep up with it. I did want to live in an organized space. I liked seeing others' homes or rooms all put together. But these basic suggestions never worked for me, and I was sure I was the problem.

Fast forward to my twenties. I had found my passion in mental and behavioral health. I became a coach and worked with people from all walks of life. I loved learning strategies that worked and being able to help others through their struggles. But like the mechanic who never fixes his own car in his downtime, my apartment and car were still a mess.

One day, the director at the organization I worked for pulled me aside and asked if I wanted to manage one of their recovery homes. I had a strong reputation at that organization. This position meant that I would be responsible for running a household where 12 residents lived. A 4000 sq. ft, 5 bedroom, 2 bathroom house meant to be a clean, healthy, structured living space for residents working on their recovery. Ensuring they made their beds, kept their rooms clean, and stuck to a regular chore schedule that contributed to the home they lived in was all part of it. Our organization had a strong 'practice what you preach' culture. Not a job I should take at this point, right?

I was in my late twenties, facing a mountain of student debt, working two jobs to keep up, and this offer came with my own separate sunny one-bedroom apartment attached to the main house. Rent-free. I said yes almost immediately.

I had no idea how I would do it, but I had to make it work. I wanted to be the person that could do well at this job for the residents' sake and for my own as well. Because this entire property belonged to the organization, we were subject to regular inspections on short notice, if any notice at all. So there was no faking it.

At this stage, I had several advantages beyond the average person with ADHD looking to get organized. First, I was freshly moving into this space, so I was mindful of what I brought with me and what got tossed. I also had time to pick the brain of the director who had managed that house for several years before me. Finally, I did a deep dive into the research to learn what made my brain different and what might help me in this scenario. Then, I started applying what I was learning and building systems and habits. Ultimately my mindset and perspective on my ability to keep things organized began to shift drastically.

Soon enough, my success at running this house was being echoed back to me at the most unexpected times. I would hear comments from residents that they were glad they were in this house compared to others. Staff would say things like, "I heard you run a tight ship over there." or, "I hear you've got a solid house."

I cannot describe how proud I was of myself. I had beyond surpassed my goal of just wanting a friend to be able to drop in for coffee unannounced. I had actually changed the way I was living. I was organized, and I was keeping it that way. I was keeping the whole house organized with 12 other people in it as well, all while still working a full-time job outside of that home.

Years after leaving that house, I still have the same systems in place. Schedules and family life have changed, but the habits I developed were both flexible and structured enough to keep me organized and proud of my home. That's my hope for you. I want you to be able to understand how ADHD impacts you and leverage the way that your brain works. I want you to establish systems and habits that make it almost effortless and help you have a home you can be proud of.

Bins, lists, and timers are all great, but I'm here to bring you the systems that work. The perspectives and habits you can put in place to start changing your life. By breaking down the science of ADHD and organization skills, sharing the stories that matter, and giving you actionable steps you can use immediately, this book is the guide you haven't seen before because it's made for you. Specifically for the person with ADHD, for you as an individual to take these strategies and make them your own.

I've spent the last several years teaching effective ADHD strategies and systems to others. In working with other adults who have ADHD, I've come to realize a few things. Many don't have a clear concept of what ADHD really is and how it's impacting them. They rarely come to therapy seeking treatment for it. It is a common misperception that the only way to address ADHD symptoms is through medication. So it can be surprising when they learn there are habits and behavioral techniques that will help.

People with ADHD often come to therapy to work on things like stress related to their home life, work performance, and academic achievement. They are coming in to talk about their anxiety and hopelessness because they can never figure out how to keep up. They explain how they struggle with laziness and want to learn how to have stronger discipline and willpower to do what they need to do.

People come in very aware that something is wrong. They can describe the impacts of their struggles in detail, and they outline their goals to be more consistent, motivated, productive, less emotionally reactive, and generally feel more in control of their lives.

At the point when they hear about ADHD, they imagine the little boy in class that can't sit still, climbs on everything, and is always disruptive. That boy was in my class too. But I sat a few rows away with symptoms that looked quite different from his.

Sometimes people will disagree that ADHD is what is going on, which often has to do with the stereotypes and stigma they perceive. Other times they remember something about having ADHD in their childhood but figured they grew out of it, and then there are the people who have a lightbulb moment, where so many things across years of time finally make sense.

It starts to click for many as they go through the diagnostic criteria. I find that the clients who do best in really changing their lives and their homes are the ones who acknowledge the problem at hand. Then they open up to genuinely learn about their brain and functioning.

Understanding the ADHD brain is key because we need a shift in our perspective and overall mindset about ourselves, our needs, and our abilities. I needed to understand that it's not just a matter of trying harder or doing the things that work for others who don't have ADHD. It's a matter of really grasping the roles of executive function and the dopamine reward pathway so that we can use strategies tailored to address these issues.

Over time I have witnessed people change their lives completely. We really underestimate the power that our home environment plays in our lives. The impact is huge! It influences the mood we wake up in, how smoothly our morning runs, and whether we leave the house feeling calm, in control, and looking forward to our day.

The habits we have at home often play out in our workspaces as well. I often see the insights and behaviors that I teach, which are aimed at the home, become generalized to other spaces that my clients spend time in, like their office or car. This is a true indicator of skill building. In these scenarios, the person is not just following and repeating instructions. They are mastering concepts and adapting them in unique ways to other situations that work.

By now, I hope it's clear that If you really want to change what is going on in your life and get your home under control, you'll need a solid understanding of what is really going on so that you can fully take in the concepts that can help. I spent a long time trying to work on my issues the wrong way. By that, I mean I had temporary success, but it never lasted.

These were like behavioral crash diets. And we know how well those work - until they don't. I could send you a beautiful picture of the room I just reorganized, but undoubtedly it would soon be back to normal. I'd be stepping over things, losing items I needed, leaving the house late because I had spent 30 minutes trying to find my keys, and losing money of all things. I would feel frustrated and ashamed. It wasn't until I learned how my brain worked and the reasons that I struggled so much that I was able to transform them into solutions that stuck.

So I'm going to walk you through that process to help you develop your own systems and solutions that stick. Once you've completed this book, you'll better understand your patterns and behavior. You'll understand how to leverage your ADHD brain and make it work for you, and you'll learn to accommodate your needs to turn your home into the stable, clean, peaceful sanctuary you deserve.

## How to use this book and what you'll learn

I've broken this book down into two parts. In the first part, you'll learn about what ADHD is, how it impacts the brain's functioning, and why it can be so damn difficult to stay organized or to motivate yourself to clean when you don't feel like it. Next, we'll cover the various practical techniques and strategies that will address ADHD issues with motivation and procrastination so that you can actually get started!

We'll have a full chapter on your step-by-step process for decluttering and staying decluttered. Clutter is a huge issue when you have ADHD. It comes back to your executive functioning. The idea of decluttering can often feel just as daunting as getting organized. By the end of that chapter, you'll have what you need to get rid of the clutter and prevent it from building back up. Then we're ready to get organized!

I'll walk you through how to establish a home organization system that works for you and that you can sustain long-term. This chapter is one of the most comprehensive in the book and guides you through how to establish a simple yet powerful organizational system based on your individual needs. You'll find that once you have developed a simple system made up of small habits, staying organized becomes automatic and easy.

Now that you've decluttered and organized, we need to keep your place clean. Cleaning is different from organizing and decluttering. This involves ongoing maintenance of your home once it's organized. People with ADHD often struggle to clean consistently and efficiently, making mistakes that waste valuable time and energy. I'm all about simplicity because I know that if it's not served up simply, it's much less likely to happen.

In the last section of Part 1, we'll talk about sustaining long-term habits. Believe it or not, there is a science to building habits! I'll tell you what you need to know about the science of building habits for people with ADHD and how you can make your new organizational system stick for good.

I encourage you to fully read Part 1 in order. I would also suggest you start practicing the concepts and strategies you are reading about and really put them into action in your own life. Try them on, see how they feel, and stick with them. I often point out to my clients that our session typically takes up about 1 hr of their week. There are 167 more hours in your week! If you only spend 1 hour reading or thinking about improvements and the other 167 practicing and reinforcing habits and behaviors that don't work for you, you are unlikely to change.

Use the key takeaways and suggestions at the end of each chapter to start making changes immediately. Don't expect perfection. Habits that stick around are built in small steps over time. We're looking for incremental tiny changes one day and one moment at a time.

In the second part of this book, I'll guide you through each room individually. You'll see short chapters for every room in your house, from the living room, bathroom, kitchen, bedrooms, etc. Each room differs in how you use it, the traffic it gets, and the best ways to get it organized and keep it that way. So we'll do a deep dive into each space, leaving no bill, pillowcase, or coffee filter unturned.

Whereas the first part of this book should definitely be read in order, in the second part of the book, you might choose to jump around depending on what suits your needs or what area of the house you want to focus on first. For example, if you don't have a home office, feel free to skip that section! But even if you have rooms in your house that are doing pretty well, I would still suggest reviewing the chapters pertaining to those rooms - you might pick up some tips you hadn't thought of!

By the time you finish this book, you'll be an expert on how ADHD affects you and your home. You'll have a strategic plan of attack to deal with it and know how to motivate yourself to action. You'll feel confident using solid approaches tailored to your ADHD brain so that you can declutter and get organized. Finally, you'll have an exact blueprint of the best strategies for each room and how to keep it all going.

# CHAPTER 1

# The Science of ADHD and Why It Makes Organizing Difficult

" Adults don't really have ADHD...."
I actually worked with a psychiatrist who had been in the field for at least two decades and said this. So I'll just say that if it's possible for some mental health professionals to feed into the stigma, stereotypes, and general misinformation about ADHD, you could have been misinformed at some point as well. So let's get aligned about what ADHD is, how it affects the brain, and what the impacts are.

For a long time, ADHD was widely thought to only affect children. The American Psychological Association defines ADHD as a neurodevelopmental disorder that can be both chronic and debilitating. It doesn't come and go, it won't disappear if we work hard enough, and although the severity and presentation of symptoms can change over time, we generally take it with us into adulthood.

Another common misconception is that males are more likely to have ADHD than females. This is based on common differences in how the symptoms present. Males are more often observed to have hyperactive, more outwardly disruptive symptoms, while females more frequently experience inattention, which can be harder to see, resulting in underdiagnosis.

People who are undiagnosed or diagnosed later in life, or even those who get diagnosed early but are given no understanding of what to expect as an adult, will struggle more with their symptoms of ADHD. We may go years feeling like we just don't measure up and wondering what is wrong with us. We might come to view ourselves as uniquely flawed in some way. But this is very much not the case.

A person with ADHD has physical differences in how their brain develops and functions. In fact, MRIs have shown consistent differences in several parts of the brain when comparing people who have ADHD and those who do not. One of the most noteworthy structures that are impacted by ADHD is the frontal lobe which is why we have significant impairments in executive functioning (Khadka et al., 2016). The executive function system generally refers to a group of mental skills we use to set goals, make plans, and accomplish things.

Additionally, we generally have less dopamine available than people who don't have ADHD (Volkow et al., 2009). This impacts our memory, motivation, mood, and feelings of satisfaction. This is why we often find ourselves chasing quick hits of dopamine by opting for fast rewards rather than being able to wait or spend time working for bigger rewards. We have a strong aversion to delaying gratification. Rewards are typically tied to motivation, and with ADHD, we frequently have a reward-motivation deficit (Volkow et al., 2009). We want the reward right now, and our preference for immediate gratification naturally makes tasks that require time and effort more difficult.

As a side note, our reduced levels of dopamine are why some people find medication helpful. The medications prescribed for ADHD tend to increase our available dopamine, thereby helping to address some of the related struggles. Though these medications do not solve our problems completely, and many people choose not to go the medication route for one reason or another. This book is both relevant and necessary whether you've chosen to use medications or not. As you've learned by now, dopamine is only one piece of the puzzle.

Knowing these differences in how our brain works and viewing our behavior through this lens can help us understand why "just try harder" and " I just need to focus" simply won't work for us. When we fully grasp the reasons behind our struggles, we can start looking toward solutions that accommodate our differences and still find ways to reach our goals.

## Why ADHD Makes Cleaning and Organizing So Difficult

So what does any of this have to do with home organization? We tend to put things down everywhere, we forget them if they're not directly in our line of sight, we stop seeing things when they sit in our line of sight for too long, and we can be impossible to motivate to action when there is no direct pressure, urgency, or reward attached to it. That's not to say that we don't want our homes to be more clean and organized, but it can feel impossible to cross the bridge from desire and intention to effective action.

When it comes to changing our behavior, knowledge is power. Knowledge builds the foundation for the strategies we need to put into practice. ADHD often makes us feel out of control, especially when it comes to simple things that we feel we should be able to do. The more we understand ourselves, the more equipped we'll be to make the changes we want to see in our lives.

So far, we've addressed common misconceptions about ADHD and explored important biological differences. Now we'll look at the behavioral patterns and challenges that stem from these biological differences and contribute to making cleaning and organizing feel like such a hopeless endeavor.

People who have ADHD typically struggle with persistent patterns of inattention or hyperactive/impulsive behaviors. They can also have a combination of both.

Inattention generally shows up as:

- overlooking details
- struggling to stay on task
- getting easily distracted or sidetracked
- having difficulty organizing tasks that involve multiple steps
- losing necessary items
- forgetting daily activities

While symptoms of hyperactivity/impulsivity include:

- fidgeting or difficulty remaining in one place
- frequent restlessness
- talking excessively

- difficulty waiting for one's turn
- interrupting or intruding upon others.

As I've mentioned, we struggle with executive dysfunction because of deficits in our pre-frontal cortex. Our executive function system is basically our brain's manager. The part that is supposed to take charge, delegate, and run the ship. Often it can feel like our manager is out to lunch. So we end up winging it and struggling to prioritize tasks effectively, identify how to approach a problem or task and decide how much time and attention we should give to things. This is why we consistently struggle with organizing, planning, managing our time, regulating emotions, and why we can often make impulsive decisions.

Working memory is a key area of the executive function system that greatly impacts our ability to maintain a clean and organized environment. Working memory is the ability to take in information and hold onto it long enough to use it. Imagine the server who takes your order without writing it down and still gets it correct. He used working memory to do that.

A working memory deficit is why I can go to the mailbox, take a look at my mail, understand quickly what needs to be addressed, decide that I'm going to address it when I get inside the house, then put it down somewhere and forget it ever existed. Even for that simple task, I easily determined the steps in my head but couldn't hold onto them long enough to follow through. In this way, working memory creates clutter and can make large tasks with multiple steps feel overwhelming and overly complicated.

Researchers also suspect our working memory impairments create the experience of time blindness (Zheng et al., 2022). Many people with ADHD do not assess time accurately. We don't correctly judge how long a task will take us, and we don't tend to accurately track how much time has passed. This, combined with difficulty focusing and a tendency to get sidetracked, lead to poor time management.

Now take that large task with multiple steps that have started to feel a bit overwhelming and combine that with our time blindness and tendency toward immediate gratification. Multiple studies have highlighted that people with ADHD struggle with delay aversion (Sjowall et al., 2013). In other words, we don't do well with delayed rewards. In fact, we avoid them. Combined, you can start to get a full picture of why we procrastinate, struggle with motivation, get easily overwhelmed, and just avoid a task altogether.

When I was younger, my stepfather could not understand why I couldn't get organized and keep things that way. He would try to incentivize me by saying, "It will just take you 2 hours, but once you're done, that's it! You'll feel so good about it and won't have to think about it anymore." Nope. First off, it would take me way longer, and I knew that. Second, delay aversion was at play. That kind of incentive made no sense to my brain because it skipped over all the misery of actually doing the organizing. I had zero capacity to think about feeling good *after* the misery was over.

Now that I've painted the picture of how entrenched our struggles are, I want to remind you that I don't struggle to keep my home organized anymore. I still have a poor working memory, I absolutely experience time blindness and delay aversion, and I experience almost every symptom of inattention and a few of the hyperactive/impulsive behaviors as well. So this is not about a magic cure-all that makes our symptoms go away. But my house is in good shape. It stays that way, and I feel good about it. The two are not mutually exclusive. We can have ADHD and still have homes we're proud of.

## You Can Have ADHD and an Organized Home

I used to say I had a butterfly brain. If you've ever watched butterflies, they seem to flutter from one flower to the next with no apparent strategy or sense of purpose, just fluttering around. You know there is a point to what they're doing ultimately, but how they go about it just looks random and like they probably could get a bit dizzy along the way. This resonated with me because it felt like my brain was constantly fluttering from one thing to the next with not much structure or purpose. I just kind of had to hope that it wanted to land on the right thing. Because when it did, I could be insanely productive.

People who have ADHD have the capacity to be highly creative because when we brainstorm, we can think of a bunch of different angles very quickly. The same mental process that makes a large task super overwhelming because of all of its daunting pieces is also the process that allows us to come up with lots of creative ideas very quickly.

The same brain that avoids tasks we might not find enjoyable and avoids working toward rewards that seem too far off will hyperfocus with intensity and precision when we find something that engages, interests, or otherwise rewards us. You've undoubtedly experienced this hyperfocus at various times. It's those moments that have you saying, "wow if I could always do this, I would get so much done!".

17

It really is about creating the right circumstances. So, while many components of cleaning and organizing a home seem difficult or nearly impossible for someone with ADHD, that may have more to do with the fact that we've been looking at the process through a neurotypical lens. We've been trying to make it work using the advice and suggestions of people who don't have ADHD.

When we start using strategies that target our struggles, we can accommodate our needs more effectively. This means addressing the limits of our working memory before we lose important information, tapping into our need for dopamine by creating a more rewarding process, and using specific strategies to reduce getting sidetracked and distracted. Developing this skill set will help you to see how a disorganized home is a side effect of not knowing how to manage certain symptoms. ADHD does not mean you inherently can't have an organized home. You just didn't have the right tools until now.

## Progress, Not Perfection – The Importance of Self-Compassion

It's common among people with ADHD to struggle with perfectionism. When combined with our challenges regulating emotions, this can quickly lead to a spiral. If left unchecked, we can go from fine to doomed in 60 seconds. Knowing this, I am very deliberate about not beating myself up. I work on the same concept with my clients. There is no benefit to holding yourself to a standard of perfection and making yourself feel shame and guilt every time you don't measure up. It still won't make you perfect. But it will make it harder for you to move forward.

Self-compassion is extremely important throughout this process. This involves acknowledging where you're at, giving yourself credit for your efforts, and accepting that you will not be perfect and that you'll likely mess up along the way. That is okay, and it's all part of the process. You can still learn from your mistakes and encourage yourself to do better as you go.

Self-compassion sounds the way you might talk to a younger sibling, a close friend, or a loved one who is going through the exact difficult moment you are having. What might you say to them, and what's the tone you would use when you say it? That's how you need to talk to yourself. We naturally have a tendency to be much harder on ourselves. Thinking that we can handle it or that it will motivate us to do better. But the truth is having ADHD has likely led to years of self-criticism and struggles with self-worth. Be mindful of the impact that being harsh on yourself will have. I want you to succeed with this. Triggering an emotional spiral by beating yourself up has the potential to stop you right in your tracks from making any progress and is simply not worth it.

I worked with a client who would regularly struggle with cleaning. Part of it was that if she thought about picking up one thing, it would spiral into thoughts about what else needed to be done in that room. Before you knew it, she created an expectation that was way beyond what she could handle at that moment. So instead of picking up one thing, which she definitely could have handled, she wouldn't do anything. She would avoid it entirely. Because in her mind, picking up one thing meant she should pick up all the things. Don't do that. Set realistic expectations. Be gentle with yourself.

I have heard many of my clients with ADHD repeatedly refer to themselves as lazy, careless, lacking willpower, etc. I assure you, these things are not the case. Ultimately, they just lacked a clear understanding of how their brain functions and responds in scenarios where people who don't have ADHD might typically be successful. When a person with ADHD tries to force those same circumstances to work by trying harder, it's not effective. This then leads to feelings of failure and self-condemnation. Once clients better understand and accept what is going on for them, they establish ways to successfully work toward their goals.

The same goes for you. It's all about realistic expectations and one small step at a time. The ultimate goal is progress, not perfection.

## Key Takeaways

- ADHD is a neurodevelopmental disorder. Symptoms persist over time and can affect all areas of a person's life.
- Understanding your symptoms helps you identify the exact strategies you'll need to reach your goal of having an organized home.
- You may have symptoms of inattention, hyperactivity/impulsivity, or both.
- Having less available dopamine impacts your mood, motivation, memory, and feelings of satisfaction. It's also why you struggle with delayed gratification.
- Executive dysfunction, caused by deficits in the pre-frontal cortex, impairs your ability to organize, plan, manage time, and regulate emotions.
- Self-compassion is extremely important throughout this process.
- We never inherently had a problem with an organized home. We just didn't have the right tools until now.

# CHAPTER 2

# Getting Started: Overcoming Common ADHD Challenges

B y now, you understand that my goal is to teach you how to use specific strategies and build habits and systems that address the ways ADHD impacts you in order to help you get and stay organized. While many books about organization will overlook the unique way a brain with ADHD functions, this book will demonstrate the importance and efficacy of working *with* your unique brain.

It all goes back to knowing how ADHD impacts you, understanding the executive function deficits and your internal reward system, and understanding that your dopamine reward system may not act the same as it would in a person who does not have ADHD. Using that lens - you can identify what about a situation is not working for you and why the thing isn't working, whether it's your working memory, motivation, difficulty organizing the task in your mind, time blindness, lack of sustained focus, etc. Once you can identify which thing it is, you can use the right accommodation to address it.

In this chapter, you'll learn simple things that can make ADHD symptoms worse, practical strategies to address common challenges, and ADHD-specific tips to get motivated, stay motivated, and beat procrastination.

# Let's Start By Not Making Your Symptoms Worse

You may have noticed you are sometimes especially distractible, unfocused, or irritable. Whereas you can go days feeling like your ADHD isn't so bad, other times, your symptoms can feel much more intense. A simple task you handled well enough yesterday just doesn't seem to be happening for you today, making you wonder what's changed.

It's essential to understand the triggers that can make ADHD even worse. Some of them you've heard before, but what can be surprising is the exact way these triggers impact your ADHD symptoms. Once we recognize the habits and circumstances that make our symptoms especially hard to manage, we can make small but necessary changes to set ourselves up for success.

## Reduce Overstimulation

Most people who have ADHD struggle with sensory processing to some degree. Meaning that we might be easily overstimulated by sensory experiences such as bright light, loud noises, and certain textures, odors, or tastes. These things can bother us to a higher degree than people who do not have ADHD and can lead to overstimulation which can leave you feeling incredibly stressed out and unable to function.

It's important to accommodate yourself. Have a set of earplugs if needed, or don't be afraid to ask a loved one to turn the volume down if it's set too high for you. Get yourself some rubber kitchen gloves if that gross texture at the bottom of the sink keeps you from going near it. If overstimulation is getting to you, don't be afraid to step away and take a breather. This is about learning to nurture yourself and the way your brain functions. In order to learn and implement some new behaviors, you can't afford to be overstimulated at the same time. Try to manage it where you can.

## Dopamine – The Link Between Exercise, Sleep, and Your Ability to Get Organized

Having ADHD means that we are already lower in dopamine than the average person. So, it makes sense that being mindful of things that impact our dopamine levels is important because we can be even more affected. That means not taking good care of our bodies can make it harder to function through seemingly simple tasks like de-cluttering the kitchen counter or putting away the laundry.

We already know that stimulant medications are among the most common treatments for ADHD. Their efficacy is due to increasing the availability of both dopamine and norepinephrine in the body. Research has clearly demonstrated that aerobic exercise also increases the availability of dopamine and norepinephrine (Mehren et al., 2020). Research also shows that the effects of exercise can be immediate. While there are many more positive long-term effects of exercise on both the brain and body, a 20-30 minute session of moderate intensity can offer immediate improvements in both cognitive and behavioral functioning for people with ADHD (Mehren et al., 2020).

Another aspect of taking care of your body is sleep. Lack of sleep will make managing your mood, focus, and working memory even worse. If you have ADHD, chances are you also have some sleep issues (Hvolby, 2015). Addressing these issues and trying to get enough sleep is super important. While the Society for Neuroscience (2008) highlights a temporary increase in dopamine following a night of sleep deprivation, they found that this is our body's attempt to compensate, and it comes with reduced cognitive functioning. So while you may still feel somewhat alert after a night of poor sleep, ongoing sleep disturbances are unsustainable for someone with ADHD and will throw you off more in the grand scheme.

This doesn't mean you have to run out and get a sleep aid. There are many other places to start. Check your sleeping environment. Consider weighted blankets, sound machines, or sleep apps. Watch your carb, sugar, and caffeine intake in the evening. Give yourself 1-2 hours away from screens before bed. There are often small changes like this that we can make to improve our sleep. And it's easy to disregard these small shifts when we underestimate the impact of meeting this basic need.

## A Word about Stress

Comprehensively addressing the topic of stress management is outside the scope of this book. But it is vital to consider whether you might have consistently high stress levels that are making your ADHD worse. Ongoing exposure to high levels of stress can further weaken the functioning of the pre-frontal cortex (Arnsten, 2015). Further impairing this part of the brain is something that people with ADHD would do well to avoid. High stress will directly impact your critical thinking abilities and can trigger your emotional dysregulation, leading to intense frustration that can be hard to calm down from. Stress will make it even harder to focus, problem solve, and organize your thoughts.

If you think you are experiencing chronic high stress, my first suggestion is to consider speaking with a mental health professional. Even if it is short-term to address the nature and cause of your current stress so that you can learn some individualized strategies. A quick search for therapists online will point you in the direction of therapists that you could speak with in person or via online therapy platforms. Therapists are more accessible now than they have ever been before, and they can help.

If therapy is not an option at this time or if you prefer to find other ways to manage your stress on your own, there are other options. The American Institute of Stress is a non-profit organization that maintains updated information on all things related to stress and managing it. They have reviewed several of the top stress management apps based on user experience and credibility. Some of their top suggestions are Headspace, Happify: For Stress and Worry, Pacifica, and ReachOut Breathe. These apps are grounded in evidence-based techniques to help you manage stress symptoms and may be useful as you continue making positive changes in your life.

# Identifying Practical Strategies that Work with Your Brain

As we move toward developing your decluttering, organizing, and cleaning systems, it is important to build the foundation you'll need to be successful in implementing those systems. Here I have identified 5 specific foundational skills that will lay the groundwork for the rest of your success throughout this book.

These skills involve developing a deeper awareness of your own behaviors to start addressing the patterns that are not working for you. You'll learn how to manage time blindness, eliminate distractions, and navigate challenges in your working memory. Finally, you'll learn the importance of assigning a specific place for important items and how to choose the right spot so that you always know where to find them.

## Recognize Your Patterns

Pay attention to the things you repeatedly do and say that cause trouble when it comes to trying to maintain a clean and organized space. This involves getting really honest with yourself about the things you are doing that are not working for you. If you can identify the ADHD challenge at hand, you can come up with more effective strategies to address it and get yourself moving in the right direction.

- Do you feel like you've been busy all day, doing things that had to get done, but you still haven't accomplished the one task you knew was important?
    - This is productive procrastination - you'll benefit from breaking up tasks, time blocking, and using anchor tasks

- Do you tend to sit there immobilized and binge-watching shows on Netflix or scrolling on social media because the idea of jumping into your task is just not something you want to do right now?
  - Your dopamine reward system would prefer to watch those shows or scroll, so you'll need to find other ways to tap into your reward system
- Do you just keep forgetting?
  - Accommodate your working memory
- Do you really want to get it done but find that you keep putting it off because you don't really know where to start or how to proceed?
  - Motivation strategies and breaking down the task into smaller pieces will help
- Do you tend to put things down in the wrong place and lack routine and structure in areas where you feel you need some?
  - This is where assigning a home for important items and using strategies to accommodate your working memory can help
- Do you tend to say unhelpful things to yourself?
  - "I'll do it in 5 minutes." - That's just a rationalization to keep doing what you are doing right now. You won't want to do it in 5 minutes, either.
  - "This is going to take forever!" - You would benefit from using strategies that target time blindness.
  - "I'll remember because this is really important." - You know your limits with working memory. If it's really important, why risk it? Write it down.

○ "I'll just write it on this scrap of paper. At least it's written, and I can add it to my planner later." - That's not going to work. You'll lose it or forget to look at it. This is a working memory issue - we have better places that are just as easy to write this down.

○ "I'll get the bedroom done tomorrow afternoon." - That's a good goal, but time blindness can make it difficult for us to accurately judge how long a task will take. Make sure you are truly giving yourself enough time.

Take a moment and think about your patterns. The moments and decisions that cause the biggest issues for you. What do they look like? What do you say to yourself? What can you do instead? This is how you recognize and address your problematic patterns.

## Managing Time Blindness

Time blindness can affect anyone but is particularly common among people with ADHD (Weissenberger et al., 2021). It goes back to our executive dysfunction issues. If you have ADHD, chances are you tend to struggle with estimating how much time a task will take you and how much time has passed once you're involved in doing the task. You'll know this is a struggle for you if you often miss deadlines, misjudge how long things will take you, or you unintentionally tend to show up too late or too early for appointments.

While time blindness does not impact every single person with ADHD, if you consider it a problem that could get in the way of getting organized or moving through tasks in your home effectively, there are several ways to start managing it.

- Add more time, even if you don't think it will take that long.
- Shut down hyperfocus when it kicks in for anything but the task at hand
- Use visual timers
- Use TV shows or music playlists as a timer
- Make the most out of small amounts of extra time in your day. An extra 5 minutes can be enough for simple tasks like checking your calendar or picking up the clutter in one room

A common mistake I see with time blindness is continuing to try the same approach and hoping it will work the next time. If you have tried a particular approach to manage your timing but find that you're continuously not meeting deadlines, taking much longer than expected, or losing track of time altogether, try one of the strategies listed above. Any strategy that helps you to be more aware of the time that is passing will help, as we can be especially present-focused when experiencing time blindness.

## Eliminate distractions

With ADHD, both internal and external distractions can pose a problem. When it comes to internal distractions, this might involve getting lost in your thoughts or daydreaming. This is a common challenge. If you are trying to listen to a lecture or meeting, you might try taking notes on what is being said. This can help keep your focus on what the speaker is saying. But when it comes to home organization, the goal is to keep your attention on the task you are engaging in.

If internal distractions are getting in your way, music can help. Research has demonstrated that our dopamine levels increase when we listen to music we like. This is why attention and focus can improve while we are listening to pleasurable music (Zhao & Toichi, 2020). There are different types of focus music; you'll have to try them out to see what works best for you. You can find them on youtube, Spotify, or focus apps. Some are just a specific type of steady sound that plays in the background of whatever you are doing. Other types of music that can help include instrumental music to help calm you or songs with lyrics. Different things work for different people, but if you find your mind wandering off too much when you are working in silence, try adding some focus music to the mix.

When it comes to external distractions, preplanning is key. Before you start working on a task, consider the potential external distractions that could come up. Phones are a common distraction, as are people around you who may not know that you need to be undisturbed. Planning ahead to prevent distractions before they occur is crucial because we may struggle to appropriately choose where our focus should be going in the moment.

For example, if you've decided to organize your closet, but your phone alerts you that an email just came through. Now you might stop organizing altogether and intensely focus on responding to that email. So it may not be that you can't focus, but more so that your focus is great - it's just not on the right thing at the right time.

We live in a time where we are used to being extremely accessible and have to handle multiple requests for our immediate attention. However, most things can wait an hour at least. Use the focus mode on your phone so that you can silence all but the most important apps for the duration of your task. For me, that looks like silencing everything but incoming phone calls for an hour at a time. If there's an emergency, I'll get a call. Anything else can wait an hour.

If others are in your house, tell them you will be busy for the next hour. Your partner might be able to help you by leaving you alone if they know you are unavailable for the next hour. If you have kids, you might set them up with a task for the next hour or ask them to help with something in particular. You could also plan certain tasks for when you know they will be otherwise occupied. This way, you have one less distraction.

## Accommodate the limits of your working memory

Some things can help address working memory deficits in the long term. Daily meditation has been shown to thicken the prefrontal cortex, which could help improve your working memory (Lazar et al., 2005). But in the meantime, acknowledge that it's an issue and make accommodations for yourself.

I've grown to expect that I will forget it and that it won't happen unless it is written down somewhere that I am definitely going to look at or unless some kind of alarm accompanies it. I actually use a few types of calendars because I want to leave myself with as little ability as possible to forget to do the things that I know are important.

It can be so much extra work to remember things that, for many people, it creates more anxiety to keep reminding ourselves of important things. Knowing that you have a place to keep those things stored can be such a relief. In that way, I don't see my planner as work but as a huge help.

I don't feel any pressure to try to remember something as long as I know I've written it down. The thing you do have to worry about is looking at it. I keep mine open and on the kitchen counter. I also use a Google calendar on my phone that will sound an alarm both 30 minutes and 10 minutes before I have to do something. Ideally, I like my written planner and Google calendar to match, but at the very least, the most important tasks I cannot forget make it into both.

I also have catchall lists. These are the lists you have running for when you don't have time or when it's not readily accessible to put the information in the ideal place, such as your calendar, planner, phone, etc. I have a whiteboard on my fridge and in my bedroom. I also use the notepad on my phone. This may sound like many lists, but they all have one function. They are a catchall for things that need to be addressed. The reason they are in 3 different places goes back to the reward system. I won't do it if it's too hard with too little reward. That includes going to another room to write something down. With this system, things always get written down.

Setting a habit of checking your lists in the morning and at night also means you won't miss anything. Don't worry if this sounds over-whelming. I've introduced the concept of habit stacking, which you can start trying and practicing now. You can check your lists in the morning by attaching them to your coffee or breakfast routine. You can also check your lists in the evening by connecting this to a specific part of your nighttime routine. We'll also do a deep dive into the science of building habits later in chapter 6.

Starting these habits of writing things down and checking them is the first step to setting up your own systems for keeping your house in shape. When you start deciding to complete certain tasks, you'll need somewhere to commit that block of time so that you don't forget. You'll need to be in the habit of checking those lists to make sure you didn't miss anything. You'll be surprised at how much less stress and pressure you feel when you realize there is no need to try remembering the next thing. I've had multiple clients tell me they didn't realize they would feel that relieved at just being able to rely on writing things down.

To make this system work for yourself, you'll need:

- A calendar app for your phone (make sure it has the ability to set alerts, such as Google Calendar).
- A planner (I prefer one that has a weekly view with hourly timeslots on each day. when it lays open, you can see one entire week)
- 2 simple whiteboards (small ones are fine)
- A notepad app in your phone (your phone likely came with one. Simple is fine)

Step 1: Let's work on your planner.

- I try to have it filled at least 2 weeks out. But if I know of other things in advance, they also get written down. Every weekend I fill in another week so that I can always see at least 2 weeks out.
- Fill in all of the appointments, meetings, events, and commitments that you currently have scheduled. (block out time needed for travel/commuting)

- Now that the MUSTs are in there, you should have a clear view of what time is available.

- Now, you'll see the available space where you can write down things you want to accomplish, like decluttering the kitchen counter.

Step 2: Set up your phone calendar.

- Take everything you put into the two weeks on your planner and enter it into your phone calendar.

- NOTE - if there are things that repeat, you should be able to choose to make them automatically repeat on this calendar on a daily, weekly, biweekly, monthly, or custom cadence. This means you won't have to manually enter it again.

- Now set up your notifications/alerts. This should be in the settings section of your calendar. I recommend at least 2 alerts for each task - one that tells you it's coming up soon and one that tells you it's almost starting. I use a 30-minute and 10-minute reminder. My phone will sound or vibrate (depending on whether I have the sound on). You might start with these alerts, try them out, and decide if you think they need to change. I would give it 2 weeks before you decide they are too much. Initially, I felt the 10-minute reminder was pointless and irritating. When I shut it off and ended up missing a meeting despite the reminder I had received 30 minutes prior, I turned it back on, and it's been that way since.

Step 3: Your whiteboards and phone notepad

- Remember, they are catchalls. Essentially backups for when your phone calendar or planner is less convenient. Or for when you want more of a visual.

- Post one on your fridge, one in your bedroom or living room (where ever you think makes the most sense. My home office is on one side of my bedroom, so the whiteboard is in there)

- The phone notepad - this may initially sound like it doesn't make sense in light of the phone calendar - but you will have moments where you want to do something but don't have the time or mental capacity to figure out when to schedule it. Rather than not saving it at all, that is when it goes on the notepad.

- The biggest thing about the catchall lists is checking them. Morning and night to see what you can move from the lists directly into your planner/phone calendar.

Perspective is huge. People often talk about writing lists and using planners. For many, this has been unsuccessful. Part of this is based on your perspective about it. I see these things as a tool to address my working memory deficit. There is definitely a deficit here with ADHD. I'm not going to remember because I want to or because it's important. So writing it down and having it attached to automatic alarms that I don't have to set are the tools that step in where my working memory stops. This also means it has to get written right away as soon as the commitment or plan is made. Use this strategy for appointments and tasks, such as a bill that's due or when you need to set aside time to work on something, like organizing your home office.

## Find a home for important items

I know I lose things, so they need a permanent spot where they always go right back. If I don't know where to put something while I'm cleaning up, that means I haven't given it a home yet, and it's not my laziness and forgetfulness that is the issue. I just haven't given it a space to go, and I know that my mind is not great at organizing on the fly.

As you consider where to create permanent spots for things in your home, you will need to acknowledge when something is not working. This is always better than trying to force it to work. Building a habit is one thing, but if it genuinely feels like it's not going to work, you might need a different system.

My keys are a great example. They've had a few different homes, but only one has worked. I tried keeping them in my briefcase, which seemed to make sense. I figured as long as they were in there, I would always have them when leaving the house. This didn't stick because they would fall to the bottom, and I would have to find them, which would take a couple of minutes. Ultimately I would get annoyed and stop throwing them in my briefcase because I didn't want to have to deal with digging them out again. Next, I tried to give them a home in a basket on the kitchen counter with other miscellaneous items. The same problem again was that other things went in this basket, the keys weren't visible, and I stopped using the system without even thinking about it. What finally worked? Key hooks. Visible, easy to find, and easy to hang there when I get home. Perfect spot, and it stuck. The point is, don't be afraid to make tweaks to your system. Just because the first home you find for something doesn't work, that does not mean you can't follow a system. It means that a particular system does not work for you. It's a combination of building the habit and choosing the right strategy.

Be flexible with yourself. I have never thought of myself as a structured person. In fact, being structured seems daunting to me. But I genuinely appreciate the hooks for my keys. I love the file holder for my papers that need to be addressed and the fact that I have a routine for when and how I go through that file because it makes my life easier. These are accommodations that work for me. As you start using the strategies I've introduced, and as we continue deeper into this book, you learn to create the accommodations that work for you.

## Get Motivated – Let's Talk About Your Why

Discovering your ultimate reason why is huge. For me, my initial reason why tapped directly into my reward system. If I kept things clean and organized, I could keep my apartment. I also had a fear of embarrassment. Knowing this wasn't a situation where I could get away with just not inviting people over, I had no choice but to accept that people might see my apartment from time to time and that I had to be prepared for that to happen on short notice. Aside from that, I very much wanted to practice what I preached. I knew I was in a position to help others, and I owed it to them to hold myself to the same standards. I did not feel good about telling the clients in that house to live one way if I was living another way. So that was my initial reason why, and it was strong enough to work.

After that, my reason became being able to enjoy when others could come over on short notice for dinner or coffee. The feeling that I got when I could just say yes or invite them felt great to be able to do something so "normal" and not to feel like I had to hide or like having friends over was off limits for me as it had been for so long before that. Nowadays, my why is my daughter. She deserves an organized space to live in rather than a chaotic one. She's more likely to run, jump, and dance around the living room when there is ample clear space for her to do so. She's more likely to play with her toys when they are clearly organized so that she knows where she can find things, and I love being able to provide that for her.

We will talk about day-to-day motivation, but I urge you to explore your bigger-picture motivation outside of that. We want an overarching motivator. Something that encompasses why you even picked up this book to begin with. Why does keeping your home and space organized matter to you? What is your bigger picture goal, the thing that drives you, the thing that you look forward to or feel proud of? That is your why.

## Tap into Your Reward System

We need to make the process of cleaning or organizing extremely quick, easy, and instantly rewarding. It needs to be fun. Research shows that behaviors are more sustainable when they are enjoyable *during* the process, not just for the reward afterward. This is something that is especially true for people with ADHD when the concept of a reward after is usually not enough to get us going anyway. We have to find reasons to like it during the process. This may involve exploring a few different ideas that feel rewarding to you.

Put on a playlist that you enjoy. Play one of the 20 podcasts or e-courses that are currently in your queue to listen to. Or video a friend while you're cleaning and organizing. I almost always call a friend while I'm doing my dishes. I do this because I can prop my phone up on the windowsill above my sink, and staying in the conversation makes the dishes go by faster and keeps me standing near the phone. It's a running joke with my friend that I only call her when I'm doing the dishes - but it works for me, and it's become so automatic that when I start to do the dishes, I then remember to call her.

It really is all about accommodating yourself.

Once you know to pay attention to your own rewards, it won't be hard to come up with ideas. There are things that naturally boost our dopamine. Sweets, for example. So you might try a healthier sweets option to munch on while you are going through storage cabinets. Upbeat music is another mood booster. Or music from your past is another often-overlooked mood booster that can immediately energize you. I will often play the 80s or 90s music while I'm cleaning.

Mirroring is another strategy that works for people who have ADHD. If you have a friend or family member who has been wanting to get their place in order, you might try scheduling with them to do it simultaneously. Then you can have them on video. Seeing them working in their own space will make it easier for you to move forward with your own task at the same time.

The Pomodoro technique is another productivity strategy that can help us make up for low motivation. It also works by breaking down a larger task into smaller pieces which feels less daunting for us. This strategy works by setting a timer for 25 minutes where you just focus on doing that one task while minimizing other distractions. Once you hit 25 minutes, you can take a 5-minute break to do whatever you want. Ideally, you should do 3-4 pomodoros, and then you can take a half-hour break.

The main takeaway from these strategies is that they aim to be simple and practical. They are also individualized. You can easily tie each of them to the challenges and struggles outlined in the first chapter, but it is up to you to identify which struggles are the biggest barriers for you and, therefore, which strategies will be your go-to. When you consider your needs through the lens of how your brain is working, figure out which things you need to make accommodations for.

If the task is too overwhelming, then break it down by writing the steps in order, then practice mono-tasking - which means one task at a time. Your only job and your only concern at that moment is the one small task rather than the whole larger job. If you're not motivated because it's too boring and tortuous, then figure out what other thing you have been wanting to do that you could combine with this task to keep you entertained and rewarded. Another example of a reward in this scenario could be that you haven't gotten to read for fun in a while. So you download an audiobook that you only play while you are doing the tasks you need to do. This adds motivation and reward to the task because you want to see what happens next in the book.

It comes back to mindset. You are not forcing yourself to suddenly become an organized person who loves structure and cleaning. You are using what you know about how you function and how your brain operates so that you can leverage those things to meet the goals that you have.

# Stay Motivated – Even When You Don't Feel Like It

Try not to get lost in the details. ADHD doesn't mean we simply can't or don't pay attention. Our difficulty is regulating which things we give attention to and how much attention we give those things. This explains why we can get quickly overwhelmed and demotivated when we consider a task that someone else might consider simple.

It is crucial to understand the kinds of things that can kill your motivation when you have ADHD. Things like a task feeling too overwhelming, lacking any immediate reward, and chasing perfection commonly lead to demotivation with ADHD. Here we'll talk about strategies that address these specific areas of motivation to help you keep the motivation going even when you don't feel like it.

Onions have layers, and so should your cleaning habits. One of your general rules should be to keep your floors and surfaces clear. Your surfaces are any other flat surfaces in the room where you might otherwise have a tendency to put things. This can include tables, counters, tv stands, couches, chairs, etc. Floors get prioritized above surfaces, but surfaces are super important as well. This way - you can walk without tripping, and it makes the whole room appear less overwhelming.

Remember, if something looks too big to address, we shut down. So keeping things off the floor and keeping your surfaces clear, even if that means your drawers or baskets are not organized, is okay. That's better than the alternative of leaving everything out everywhere until you have the time or motivation to actually organize it, which will never come if you take that approach.

So, think of it in layers. Your first layer is just getting things off the floor. Next, get the things off the surfaces. Having clear floors and clear surfaces feels better. It can be counterintuitive to just move it so that it looks cleaner even if it's not fully organized, but we already know that when you feel better, you feel naturally more motivated. This automatically triggers your reward system, making you feel a sense of accomplishment.

Then the next layer is to choose a drawer or a bin to go through. One at a time. But at least your room looks and feels better and is ready to go. As long as your most important items have homes - such as your keys, wallet, phone, checkbook, etc. These things need forever homes. Once those spots are established, you clean in layers so that you can keep moving forward without being overwhelmed. You're not losing important things you need, your home feels better, and the concept of organizing feels like something you can actually do because when you look around, it looks and feels clean!

# Beat Procrastination

We procrastinate on things when we really don't want to do them. A couple of reasons could be at play here. One is that you might not have tapped into your reward system. So the task itself doesn't feel incentivizing, and even if you know rewards will come, that's still not strong enough to get you moving. The other possibility is maybe you want to do it but feel like you have no idea where to start because the task itself feels too big and overwhelming. Let's talk about breaking things down.

## Extremely Small Steps

When you are struggling to organize the steps in a way that makes sense to get the thing done, this is an executive function issue. While this book will break down many tasks for you by giving you step-by-step and room-by-room instructions to declutter and get organized, it's an important skill to develop for anyone with ADHD to be able to break things down to make them more achievable.

When approaching a larger task involving multiple steps, you want to break it into extremely small parts. At any given time, you are just doing that one small thing rather than the whole big thing.

For example, if you need to change the sheets and make the bed:

- Find and grab a fitted sheet, flat sheet, and pillowcases
- Bring them to the bedroom
- Strip everything off the bed until you get to the mattress
  - Put the clean blankets/pillows on a chair, top of a dresser, end table, etc.
- Put the fitted sheet on the bed
- Pull off the old pillowcases
- Put on new pillowcases
- Put the pillows on the bed
- Flat sheet on the bed
- Blanket(s) on the bed
- The bed is done!
- Everything that's left over goes into the laundry basket

For each step, you're just focused on that one small thing while reminding yourself that it's just going to take a few seconds or minutes.

The more you normalize how small the steps are and how fast they will go, the less daunting this task is, and the less you are likely to procrastinate doing it. When you break things down like this, you are just committing to the next small step. You are avoiding feeling overwhelmed by having tunnel vision on only that one small thing. Then you move on to the next thing.

## Using an anchor task to beat productive procrastination

Productive procrastination is when we do beneficial things that need to get done while putting off the more important task that we really should be doing at that time (Steel, 2011). Having an anchor task can help with this. You might be more likely to use productive procrastination while attempting to clean or organize a particular room. Choose an anchor task for that moment knowing and expecting that you might get sidetracked. If it's identified as your anchor task, you always return to it. It's your anchor.

So if you want to clean the kitchen, part of that is doing the dishes. If you're unloading and loading the dishwasher, you might get sidetracked several times - "Oh, I just thought of this - let me do that real quick - or let me write this down." A family member might come in and wants help with something, or perhaps your phone rings or an email comes through. Whatever the sidetracking things are, remember that while you expect a certain amount of distractions will happen, the dishwasher at that moment is your anchor, so you come back to that.

Using an anchor task means it's okay if your attention and focus are not naturally sustained, and you allow the tiny breaks as long as you return. Anything larger that takes more than 2-3 min is something you can write down quickly and come back to complete after the anchor task is done. Once that anchor task is finished, you can choose the next anchor.

## Committing to small blocks of time

When you're really struggling with procrastination, it helps to commit to an extremely small amount of time. With this strategy, you're not committing to an entire task or even a portion of a task. Rather, you're saying, "I'll give this 5 minutes."

When you commit to doing a tiny amount of time, that at least gets the ball rolling. We struggle with time blindness, so we don't accurately judge how long things will take us. You might think, "I could get this done in 2 hrs." Yet after 2hrs have gone by, you might still not be at the halfway point. Likewise, you could feel like something will take forever. Meanwhile, it could get done in 20 minutes.

So when you are struggling with motivation and telling yourself, "This could take forever.", commit to doing it for 5, 10, or 15 minutes. Whatever *small* chunk of time will get you moving. Set your timer and do the thing for that amount of time with maximum effort. When the timer goes off, ask yourself:

"How do I feel about what I just got done"

"Can I do that again?"

If so, give it the same amount of time with another short burst of focus. This works for a few reasons. We have taken away the daunting element of it taking forever and only committed to a time that we were okay with. We also trigger your reward response when we ask how you feel about what you just got done. This involves taking a little step back, assessing your progress, and triggering that sense of a reward and that dopamine hit, which will help you be more likely to say yes, I'll go for another chunk of time.

Now it's important to realize that you are not committing to a full hour or to completing the entire task. Rather you are just committing to that tiny amount of time, and you still have the full right to say, "no thanks, I'm done.". Decide when you might ask yourself again to do another 5-10 min. Maybe again that night, or maybe try again at the same time the next day? This is a great strategy for chipping away at an otherwise large task that might have never gotten done.

Struggles with motivation, time blindness, procrastination, focus, working memory, etc., are common challenges with ADHD. You may find that some of these challenges play more of a role than others or that the primary challenge differs depending on the type of task you need to do. Having an awareness of your core struggle at that moment will help you better identify which practical strategy will be most useful so that you can ultimately succeed in maintaining a clean and organized home.

## Key Takeaways

- Drops in dopamine have a strong impact on your symptoms and your ability to function
- Minding your exercise, sleep, stress, and overstimulation will help you to stay functioning at your best
- It is crucial to recognize your patterns and how they contribute to the problem
- Time blindness is a common challenge with ADHD, but there are practical ways to manage it.
- Eliminating distractions is difficult but necessary
- Mitigate both internal and external distractions to keep your focus

- A simple system involving a planner, calendar app, whiteboards, and alarms combined with habitual checking of these lists and calendars can help make up for working memory deficits
- Important items need to be assigned specific and consistent places in your home
- Motivation starts with identifying your 'Why'
- Motivation continues by tapping into your rewards system, accommodating yourself, and breaking things up into small manageable pieces.
- Anchor tasks, time blocking, breaking things down into extremely small steps, and tapping into your sense of accomplishment can help beat procrastination.

# CHAPTER 3
# Habit Building for People with ADHD

Building habits is hard for us. People with ADHD are generally inconsistent and struggle with sticking to routines (Carr-Fanning, 2020). By nature we tend to have a low tolerance for boredom, we crave novelty, we are driven by immediate rewards and have lower than average impulse control. Not to mention, we can be a bit forgetful. So, while we know that routine and structure are good for us, they are also something we have likely never been naturally good at.

While you know building habits may not be automatic for you, it will be a necessary skill as you work to clean up, get organized, and keep things that way. After all, you've likely been able to get things looking neat and organized once or twice before, but your difficulty keeping it that way is one of the reasons you're reading this book now.

## Choosing the Right Strategies for You

There are many strategies out there that promote habit formation and that are designed to help people create a routine and stick with it. Some of them are more ADHD friendly than others. One of the books that you will see ADHD coaches refer to across the board is *Atomic Habits* by James Clear (2018). His strategies are ADHD friendly because they hone in on some of the biggest struggles we have with habit building.

Clear points out that if you are having difficulty building a habit, it is likely your system that needs work and not some inherent flaw in your character. He emphasizes the importance of the reward system, not only after the task is completed but throughout the entire process. Additionally, he acknowledges and even frames in a positive light the concept that we typically lean toward the path of least resistance, and that this is an evolutionary strength.

If you're new to *Atomic Habits* this chapter offers a great introduction to some of the main components in Clear's framework, while delivering additional strategies developed with an ADHD brain in mind.

The most important thing when adopting strategies to build habits is to choose the ones that work for you. Have a sense of what your biggest downfalls are when you've tried to build habits before, and pick techniques that address these issues. Try things out and don't be afraid to adjust until you create a system that suits your individual needs. While having ADHD means we are likely to have common struggles and similar responses to certain sets of circumstances, we are still individuals and our presentations of ADHD symptoms will differ.

## Understand your Goals

This is where the rewards process begins. Does "I want to clean my kitchen regularly" sound like a rewarding goal to you? When it comes to ADHD we are highly motivated by immediate rewards. We are also easily shut down by things that sound mundane or that don't entice us enough.

How about "I want to start my morning strong, feeling confident and in control of my day". That sounds like something you might actually want right? Tap into what your real goal is. You can get there by taking your boring goal and asking "Why?" or "What will it do for me?". If I were to ask you "Why do you want to clean your kitchen regularly?" or "What is a clean kitchen going to do for you?" This is how we got to the idea of starting strong and feeling confident and in control of your day.

Clear (2018) points out that our primary rewards are things like food, water, and sex. Secondary rewards are also powerful motivators. These can include things like money, power, praise, approval, status, personal satisfaction, friendships, and love. If you consider the goal above, it taps into the rewards of power, personal satisfaction, and if I want to be perceived as this person who is strong, confident, and in control, I also tap into the need for approval and potentially praise from others. It's very likely that if you have goals you really want to accomplish, they are linked to these primary or secondary rewards. Dig until you find that connection. That reward is the foundation of your ultimate goal, your hook, the initial piece of motivation that will move you to take action.

## Be Specific

Now that you've identified your goal, you need to be specific about the action you want to take. This will ultimately lead into the habit you want to establish. If I want my mornings to start off strong so that I'm feeling confident and in control of my day, being able to make and enjoy my morning coffee is a big part of that.

I don't want there to be any friction in that part of my morning. I want it to run smoothly so that I barely have to think and I can move through the motions fluidly to the point where I can stare out my window drinking that hot cup without feeling pressured, or stressed in the process.

I could go in a few different directions with actions that would be conducive to this. One thing I know I'll need is to have the coffee area in my kitchen to be organized, clean, and ready to go without having to rummage around for the sugar or clean out the coffee filter. Everything should be ready.

So my specific action could be taking 5 minutes to quickly clean and prep my coffee station before I close down the kitchen each night. To make it even more clear, this includes wiping down the area, making sure coffee mugs are clean and available, and making sure there is no clutter in my way. The coffee scoop is where it needs to be on the side of the machine, the sugar and coffee are in the cabinet nearest to the machine, the coffee filter is clean, the water tank is filled.

This prep takes all 5 minutes at most. The next part of creating a clear and specific task is to decide when it will be done. This depends on what works best for you. You might want to set a specific time to wrap up the kitchen and prep your coffee station, meaning that an alarm goes off at 8pm to signal you to complete this task. Or perhaps an alarm goes off that signals you to do a few things that help you shut down your home for the night. Another method to decide when to complete this task is habit stacking.

## Habit Stacking

There are already things that you do on a daily basis. Simple habits that you have as part of your normal activities of daily life. Habit stacking is when you associate the new habit you want to create with things you already do regularly.

These things include:

- brushing your teeth
- taking a shower
- getting dressed and undressed
- having lunch
- ending the work day
- walking into a room for the first time that day
- walking out of a room for the last time that day
- turning off the lights

This is a good moment to take note of the things you do daily. There are likely more things you can add to the list above. Any of these daily habits you already have can be used to habit stack.

For example, if every evening you check the door to make sure it's locked before you turn off the lights, this could be where you add the habit of your 5 minute coffee area prep. By making sure your door is locked and turning off the lights, you are signaling to yourself that your use of the kitchen is done for the night. So this time might make sense to ensure you are ready for the morning and the next that you will be doing in that room. Which will be to enter the kitchen and start making your morning coffee.

When it comes to establishing new habit stacks, write them out for yourself. Clearly. Include what you will do and when you will do it. Then when you completed it, take a brief step back, look at your work, and check it off your to do list. Accomplishing something you set out to do and acknowledging that by assessing the good job you did is also inherently rewarding. You want to keep the reward system engaged.

## Start Small and Build from There

I'm sure you noticed the task that I chose to create for building our new habit was pretty small. This is another aspect of Clear's framework that makes it so ADHD friendly. We are unlikely to engage in something if it feels too big or overwhelming. If you recall the strategies to beat procrastination, one of them was breaking things down into very small parts. The same applies when you are building a habit.

If you recall the goal of starting the morning strong, so that I feel confident and in control of my day, this is not something that is solely associated with my morning coffee moment. When you hear that goal, and try to picture it, you likely see an entire kitchen. It looks nice, smells nice, it's bright, devoid of clutter, and everything is in its place. That makes sense!

But here is where I caution you to start small. You don't want to set a task that you are likely to feel overwhelmed by or procrastinate on. So if your mind jumps to a beautiful, perfectly organized kitchen, this is where you break it down. I chose one small yet important moment of my morning that takes place in the kitchen and created the task based on that.

Once the task you have set out to do starts to feel simple and easy, you build on it. So in a week or two if the task I chose has started to feel easy and automatic, that's when I might add scanning for any clutter that needs to be put away or wiping down all the kitchen counters and table.

## Make it Work for *You*

Routines and habits should work for you based on your specific lifestyle, preferences, and what you find to be rewarding and motivating. Don't choose routines or habits solely because it feels like what you should be doing. That is a fast track to habit failure. The habit you develop needs to resonate and make sense for you.

If you're a night owl and you like the idea of an 11pm session of sweeping and mopping your kitchen floor while listening to an audio book you've been wanting to check out, that's great! If you tend to go to bed early but you like the idea of waking up early to listen to music and set your mood for the day while going through each room decluttering from the night before, that works too!

Your routine doesn't have to make sense to anyone else. It just has to work for you and your household.

Listen to yourself. Make space for what you like and what you don't like. Acknowledge that certain times of the day are more productive for you. Be okay with trying out the new routine or habit and be open to shifting it if it feels like it's not working.

## Be Flexible

One of the quickest ways to fall off your newfound habit is to have rigid expectations. Be willing to adjust if needed. If you find that a habit is just not working, don't use that as a reason to beat yourself up. Rather use it as information. It signals that something isn't working here and we need to consider a different approach.

Watch out for perfectionism, find ways to make the task more fun and enjoyable, and give yourself positive feedback and grace during this process. If this was something that came easy to you, you would have done it a long time ago. You are working on figuring out the system that works best and sometimes, that is not readily obvious.

You also don't have to accomplish the task every day for it to be successful. You can aim for daily, but know that you are still making progress even if you fell off for a few days that week. Try to set a rule for yourself, such as 3 strikes and you're out. Aim to check it off daily. Ultimately, if you only completed the task 2-3 days that week, that's way more than before you tried to establish the routine at all! Aim to build the frequency as you go, but if you hit 3 days where you have not been able to complete the task, then consider what you can change to make it work better for you.

## Change it Up

Another component of adding flexibility is that maybe your routine does work in the beginning. Maybe you notice that you tend to do great with the routines and habits you are establishing for 2 weeks or a month, and then it starts to fall off. Does this mean it didn't work?

It's likely that if you started strong with a routine and you were able to stick to it for a few weeks before you started falling off track, the habit started to become boring. We crave novelty and spontaneity. This is an excellent place to allow for flexibility rather than trying to force it to stick. It's pretty common that we'll love something initially and then quickly become bored and done with it.

You can still accomplish the tasks that need to get done without having to commit to one schedule forever. The house I ran had a weekly rotation of household chores. We met on a weekly basis, and in the last 10-15 min, everyone looked forward to changing up the routine. If one person did the kitchen this week, maybe she chose the living room the following week, and so on. This concept of novelty exists in various areas of our lives, and we can leverage it when it comes to our household tasks. If you follow sports, it's exciting when a new season comes up. If it were basketball all year, you'd probably get bored. It's more exciting when you can go from basketball to baseball to football. Or if you've gone to college, you know it can be exciting when a new semester starts. Still the same task of going to class, doing homework, and taking midterms, but the change can be initially invigorating.

When it comes to applying this kind of flexibility in your household tasks, it is essential to strike a balance between structure and flexibility. For example, you wouldn't start keeping your keys in a different location once you've found a spot that works. That will just make you more likely to start losing them again. The combination of effort, time, and boredom puts us in the danger zone.

To address your need for spontaneity, you'll change those tasks that require some of your time and attention but no longer feel interesting in the way you are doing them. So instead of doing the laundry every morning, you might decide to do it right after work every day. Instead of going through your paperwork on Sunday mornings with your coffee, you might decide it feels nicer to let yourself have that morning coffee to just relax and reflect. So, you'll do the paperwork while having a smoothie and listening to music on Wednesdays during your lunch break. Same task but a very different vibe.

You might thrive on changing up aspects of your routine on a weekly, biweekly, or monthly basis. Or you can challenge yourself to see how long it works before you start missing days and then use that as your signal to come up with a new one. Building habits doesn't have to mean extreme rigidity. The more flexible you can be with yourself, the easier it will be to stick to your decluttering, organizing, and cleaning systems.

## Make it Rewarding All the Way Through

Remember the importance of establishing a system that is rewarding. You learned about the role of the dopamine reward system in previous chapters, and we touched on the role of rewards in the habit building process earlier in this chapter.

Your ultimate goal is based on a primary or secondary reward that triggers your motivation to act. While you are completing the action, you can make that process enjoyable and rewarding as well. This is where music, podcasts, phone calls with friends, audio books, your favorite cup of tea, etc. come in. Finding ways that you can incorporate other things you really like at the same time as your task to build an association between the two will make you less likely to avoid doing the task.

Assessing the outcomes of your work is another way to reward yourself, as well as using positive self talk along the way. Being gentle with yourself and giving yourself credit for the progress you are making even if it's not perfect end goals. It's all about making progress one small step at a time.

Finally, find a way to reward yourself after you've completed the task. You don't have to do this for every task, but if you have one that you think might require a bit of an extra incentive then this is where the reward comes in to acknowledge your completion of the task.

Consider things that you personally find rewarding. Maybe a full week of completing the habit means you can order in from your favorite restaurant. Perhaps a month of daily completion means you can grab yourself tickets to a basketball game. You can even consider paying yourself for your hard work. Maybe each day that you accomplish this task means $5 or $10 more in your recreation/entertainment budget for the month. Consider what you really like or want and find ways to use them to reward yourself.

Each time you have completed a task, don't forget to check it off. If on your calendar or in your planner, you can start to see a string of completions indicated by little green check marks, or whatever symbol you'd like, that feels like success! Clear supports this concept as well. Seeing those little checks can be an intrinsic reward as you start to feel proud of yourself for consistently accomplishing what you set out to do.

## The Only Failure is When You Stop Trying Altogether

You will fall off track. But this doesn't mean the habit is dead. Try not to beat yourself up. A quick way to kill a habit before you've even gotten a chance to establish it is to associate it with lots of guilt and shame. That's essentially what you are doing if you beat yourself up every time you fall short.

We are immediate gratification driven, we can be impulsive, and we tend to struggle with regulating our emotions. Recognize that you are trying and that this is a work in progress. If you make this something extra unenjoyable because it makes you feel bad about yourself, you'll be more likely to toss it out the window, never to be attempted again.

Rather, give yourself credit for the strides you make. Be gentle with yourself. And if it is repeatedly not working, be willing to see what you can do differently, bringing back our concept of being flexible.

## Apply What You've Learned

Remember what you know about how ADHD works. It is highly un-likely that everyone will be successful the first time around with these strategies. There is nuance to them. There are ways that you need to individualize them for yourself and that may be a bit of a learning curve for you. That is totally okay.

Also keep in mind the strategies that you've learned to beat procrastination and improve motivation. There were several skills and techniques brought up in those areas that may also need to be applied when it comes to developing habits.

## Use Your Resources

Your resources include all of the tools at your disposal. I've mentioned several so far. These include planners, lists, white boards, alarms, notepads, apps, music, etc. Even your supports are a huge resource in this process. You have access to all of these and you need to use them as they can fit with your individual needs, lifestyle, and the routine you are building.

Many of these tools will help with forgetfulness and will assist you to establish consistency. They can also be used in the mentally rewarding process of tracking and recording your wins and progress. Additionally, if you struggle with prioritizing and organizing tasks in your mind, using these tools will help with mapping things out in a way that makes sense and give you a visual aid so that you can better conceptualize your plan.

Your support system can be useful in a number of ways. It's helpful when you have a good sense of who is in your corner and how they can each best support you. You may have that friend who is your best cheerleader to encourage you along the way and praise your accomplishments. You may have that person who has their own cleaning or organizing goals and may want to act as a body double so that you both can be on video motivating one another by doing your routines together.

## Accountability

Supports can also be an accountability system. You may feel a greater sense of accountability to accomplish a task once you have told a member of your friends or family that you will be doing that thing. In this case just be careful to not choose supports who may make you feel bad if you don't accomplish the task or who won't understand the importance of being able to adapt your routine to better suit you. Encouragement is great! Shame and guilt are not helpful here.

Make sure to consider all of the tools and resources at your disposal and choose how and when you will use them in your process. They can each go far in helping you develop your system and accomplish your overall goals.

# Key Takeaways

- Habit building is harder for people with ADHD, but can be accomplished by choosing ADHD friendly strategies
- Identify the ultimate goal, this means understanding the connection to your primary or secondary rewards
- Write down your new habit being as specific and clear as possible to reduce avoidance, forgetfulness, or procrastination
- Use habit stacking wherever possible, by attaching new habits to your already existing habits
- When it comes to building habits, start really small and build on to it as the habit gets easier and more automatic
- Your habits and routines don't need to work for other people, they need to work for you
- Be flexible, if something is not working you can change it at any time

- Use the reward system throughout the entire process, from start to finish

- Don't beat yourself up, we want progress, not perfection. When something doesn't work, that's information you can use.

- Don't forget everything you've learned about how ADHD works and what that means for you, including tips to address procrastination and low motivation

- Use the resources and tools at your disposal. That's what they're there for!

# CHAPTER 4

# Decluttering with ADHD: Clearing the Mess, One Doom Pile at a Time

One of the most significant barriers to getting organized is often the clutter that sits in the way of it all. Making actual organization feel close to impossible. As you've begun to learn in this book, executive function deficits can do a number on people with ADHD. When you combine our poor working memory, weak impulse control, and lower levels of dopamine, it's no wonder we struggle with clutter! These issues are at the core of how ADHD impacts our brains differently from people who don't have ADHD and why we often have such a hard time organizing our tasks and our environments. People commonly struggle with clutter to the extent of feeling like achieving organization is an insurmountable goal.

As we have explored and outlined earlier, our challenges can absolutely be overcome. That is not to suggest our symptoms will be cured by the strategies presented here. Rather we can mitigate their impact on our lives. Once we learn to leverage what works for us and work around the triggers that throw us off in a strategic way, we learn that a clean and organized space is something that we can achieve.

## Didn't Organize, Only Moved

If you've seen any discussion of ADHD struggles and behaviors on social media lately, you've probably heard of doom piles. There are also doom boxes, doom bags, and even doom rooms. These are clusters of items that, rather than organizing, we just piled all together. Imagine the classic junk drawer that even organized homes have. Except we've got lots of these, in various forms and sizes throughout our home, taking up space on counters, chairs, tables, bags, bins, drawers, and even entire rooms.

Doom stands for 'didn't organize, only moved.' That's how these piles came together, and it's also an excellent way to describe the feeling you might have when trying to deal with these areas of clutter. Not only do these areas make it less likely that you can find what you are looking for, but they also make your space more congested. Clutter like this often leads you to have to step over things, it takes up space on a chair that you would otherwise sit at, or fills up a counter or tabletop that you would otherwise use but can't because things are in the way.

When your home environment is in a constant state of clutter, it can wreak havoc on many areas of your life. Clutter can be the reason your morning starts out feeling scattered and stressed. You've likely had mornings where you can't find your keys, you spend half an hour trying to find what you intended to wear, and you can't find the AirPods that help you stay focused while you're working. Whether you go to work or work from home, it can lead to moments of embarrassment in front of your colleagues, boss, or clients when you can't find something they ask you for that you were supposed to have. Even worse, perhaps you forget to do something because you lost track of the post-it note you wrote it on.

Then after a stressful day of work, your dopamine is even further depleted, and the last thing you want to do is clean or organize anything. At this point in the day, if you don't have a system, it's very easy to just keep adding to the clutter, making it a vicious cycle. This extent of clutter can make you feel out of control, stressed, anxious, depressed, and further isolated because, frankly, it's an embarrassing problem that many people with ADHD tend to shame themselves about.

## How Did it Get this Bad?

As I've mentioned, working memory plays an important role here, and our deficits in working memory are largely responsible for our issues with clutter. Because we don't already have a solid organization system, things in our house can easily go from being held in our hands to being set down on the next available surface, wherever that might be. Surfaces that accumulate clutter can include the floor, couch, bed, desk, counters, tables, tv stands, shelves, and chairs. Essentially any flat surface that can hold a thing is likely to accumulate clutter in a house belonging to a person with ADHD.

Once we have it in our hands and don't need it anymore, we don't know where exactly to put it at that moment, and we might even try to help ourselves out by deciding, "I don't want to forget this," or "I don't want to lose this." So we might put it down in an *extra safe* place, which we promptly forget, or we intentionally leave it in sight because we are confident that this will lead us to address it later. You know how that story ends. A good amount of your clutter likely consists of things you left out to address later.

Another fun thing about clutter and ADHD is that we have a tendency to stop seeing it. Many have reported becoming so accustomed to their clutter that it starts to feel and look normal, so there is even less incentive to get rid of it or get it organized. In these cases, the clutter may as well be part of the furniture because it no longer looks like or feels like a task that needs to be addressed.

Impulsivity is another significant factor. It's no secret that people with ADHD can struggle with impulse buying. We often buy things we don't need, further adding to the clutter in our homes. This is related to both our lack of control over inhibitions as well as our old friend dopamine. We love immediate gratification, and a new purchase is sure to give us that quick feel-good boost we needed. So, part of our system to stay decluttered once we have cleared the chaos is to be deliberate about controlling our impulse buys. We have to stop accumulating things we don't need.

Finally, while you may have decluttered and organized tons of times before, up to now you have likely had a really hard time being consistent. I have zero doubt that you have gotten areas of your home or even your entire home beautifully decluttered and organized at one point or another - only for it to fall back to its old messy ways - and the first slip down that slippery slope was the clutter, one piece at a time. That one piece of paper, that empty water bottle, the post-its, the items that legitimately felt like they had nowhere else to go at that moment or that you told yourself you would take care of soon. Except, they just stayed there, the area got worse, and before you knew it, the clutter and mess were back with a vengeance.

## But There is Hope

On the flip side, gaining control over your clutter can make a massive difference. Freeing your space from the chaos and being able to move about freely, using the space in your home as it was intended, and finding the things you need when you need them can make your day better from the get-go. When you can make sense of your environment in this way, you won't be scrambling to get ready to leave the house, forgetting things you needed, and you won't be embarrassed to have friends and family come over. This seemingly small change can significantly improve your life, productivity, efficiency, and overall sense of well-being.

## Reiterating the Foundation

In previous chapters, we emphasized the importance of having a home for your most important things. This refers to the 4-5 items you need to use on a regular basis and cannot or prefer not to leave the house without. These are the things that, when you lose them, can literally stop you in your tracks or ruin your day. This can include your wallet, keys, planner, earbuds, phone charger, or anything else that is integral to your daily functioning - I'm assuming that you generally have your phone on or near you and, therefore, not including it in the list of things that need a home. But if you are not someone who always has their phone within reach, and if you tend to frequently lose it long enough to feel like it's a problem, then include your phone on this list as well.

Assigning a home for these items means storing them in the same place every day. You are giving them a place to live whenever you are not actively using them. Perhaps your keys live on the key hook near your door, while your wallet or purse lives on a specific shelf in your bedroom, and your charger is always plugged into a particular outlet in your living room or kitchen. These are just examples, but what works about them is that they remain consistent. You will get a sense of what feels like a natural place to keep these things. Anything that doesn't work can get re-assigned to a home that makes better sense for that item.

For example, you may prefer to have everything you need for the day stored in a basket on a table near your door. This may be especially true if you work outside of your home and you don't want to be walking around to different places to gather the things you'll need to go. CHADD, the leading non-profit national organization for children and adults with ADHD, refers to this type of space by the door with all the things you need to leave as a launchpad. You may find that your own version of a launchpad is exactly what you need for your mornings before leaving the house.

Once you have the important items essentially out of the way and accounted for, it's time to start decluttering. You'll start to see how the chapters and skills in this part of the book build on one another. We've covered the prerequisites for decluttering. Next, we'll learn about how decluttering your space is a necessary step before you can truly get organized.

## Where to Start

Pick one cluttered spot to work on. Don't set out to declutter your whole home or even a whole room. It's simply too much. Remember some of the simple strategies targeted at your ADHD needs in previous chapters. Breaking things down into small achievable tasks, using small blocks of time, keeping yourself motivated, and building one small habit at a time are all foundational to making real progress.

So once you have chosen your area - take a good look at it. Chances are, you often don't assess your clutter for what it consists of. ADHD makes organizational skills a challenge, and this would include your ability to look at something that is complex, messy, and comprised of lots of smaller pieces and make sense of it. Your cluttered area is essentially a blob of smaller pieces that may or may not even be related to each other. I want you to assess what categories of items you see.

Our ultimate goal is to take all of those little things and either:

- get rid of them,
- arrange them to be more neat and accessible, or
- put them somewhere else that makes sense for them to go

So first, we need to have a better understanding of what is there. Then we can start pulling them out of the pile and figuring out where they will go.

So look at your cluttered area. Remember the importance of breaking things down into small pieces. A cluttered area, in this case, does not refer to an entire room or one side of a room. Depending on the size of your room, the area you'll start with is maybe a quarter of it, if that.

It's a small area that could be one cluttered shelf, one section of the countertop, a section of the couch, or a portion of your desk. This may not sound like a lot, but when it's full of clutter, that's about as much as you might be able to work with at once. You also don't want this to feel like a huge job. It should be small enough that you can sit or stand in front of it and reach everything in front of you without having to get up or take any steps.

Now that you are focused on this little area, what do you see? Take a quick mental note, or jot it down. For example, if you're in the bedroom, you might see a bunch of clothes. That is what your cluttered section might look like, but the next step is to specify further. You might see shirts, jeans, sheets, towels, socks, etc. Do you see any other categories of things in that area? Paper? Toiletries? Office supplies? Ultimately we will want to physically take things out of the cluttered spot and form smaller piles according to the item category.

Make sure you have 2-3 garbage bags available. One is for garbage. One is for donations. One is for recyclables if you recycle. Now depending on the contents of your clutter, you may find that one type of those bags does not apply. That's fine, just keep the ones you need. But generally, those are the bags you want to have in mind or on hand when you start decluttering an area.

As you start going through the pile, you want to start putting things in these bags. Do yourself a favor and mark the bags. This way, you are not continuously having to check the contents or find that you put the wrong things in the wrong bag and end up having to work backward.

Now, in addition to these bags, you're going to make piles. The piles are for things that you will keep. They will be arranged based on what type of item they are. Do not worry about where they will go yet. Just separate them because, ultimately, we want to keep similar items together. These piles will be made up of things that will be either staying here and going back in a more needed and accessible way, or that will be going somewhere else more appropriate in the house. You don't have to have that figured out yet. Just know what they are and what their function is and start grouping them that way.

Be aware that people with ADHD can have a harder time letting go of possessions based on emotional attachments and sentimental value (Lynch et al., 2017). We can also be fans of the concept of "you never know when you'll need it." These are mindsets that contribute to clutter, and we need to be mindful of these patterns in our thinking as we are going through items and considering what to keep or not. When in doubt, let it go. If you can't make an extremely strong case for keeping the thing, chances are you really don't need it. If you haven't used it in a few years, you definitely don't need it.

For example, if you are going through clothes, follow these suggestions when you start decluttering:

## Get Larger Items Out of the Way First

If there are obviously larger items in the cluttered area, pull them out first. We're talking about prominent items that would otherwise be in the way while you are trying to sort. If you are working with clothes or laundry, this usually means towels, sheets, sweatshirts, and jeans. Larger bulkier items make your whole pile look larger and make it harder to get to the smaller things. Getting rid of these first will make the biggest and quickest dent in your cluttered area, giving you some immediate gratification in the much smaller and more manageable pile you have after only a couple of minutes of work.

## Decide Whether to Donate or Toss It

If you are debating about whether to keep an item of clothing, consider whether it is in good condition. If so, but you haven't worn it for a full year, I strongly suggest donating it. This means you have gone through all of the seasons and did not wear it. This also goes for clothes that don't fit. If they are not your current size, get rid of them. If it's in poor condition, toss it. It's just taking up space.

## "Someday" is a Clutter Buzzword

If the only reason you are holding onto it is "because I might want to wear it someday," but you cannot think of the last time you wore it, get rid of it. Reasoning like "someday" or "just in case" should set off your decluttering alarm bells.

## Sort Quickly

If you are keeping the item, quickly make a pile for it. It can be its own new pile if it doesn't fit easily with any of the others. Don't spend too long thinking about your piles or thinking about any one individual item. This will slow you down or make you stop altogether. Give the item a spot off to the side, close enough to you that you can reach it but away from the actual clutter area being addressed. As you go through the cluttered area, you are creating more piles and adding to your existing piles until they have been sorted.

This is the same process that you will use for other kinds of cluttered areas. Let's take your home office desk, for example:

- Gather your bags: donate, garbage, recycle
- Start with the most prominent items that are in the way. If there is obvious garbage lying around, get rid of that first. The same goes for water bottles or books. Essentially, start with the biggest bulkiest type of items.
- Next, go for the smaller items that might be in high quantities. For example, if you have 30 post-it notes spread across your desk, pick those up.
- Now start picking up things that are closest to you - if it's a desk or countertop and things are spread out enough - you may be able to go for things in a certain category first - for example, I'm going to grab all the pens I see, or all the paper-clips, all the random non-office things.
- If categories like that do not seem readily obvious, go for what is closest to you and move outward. Or move from one side to the other.
- However you decide to start, it should come quickly to you without much thought. Imagine you are on one of those game shows where you have to pick up things fast. Start grabbing and sorting. No thinking, no addressing anything in that pile at the moment, Just grabbing and sorting.
- You might even add the time-blocking component and give yourself a challenge by saying, "I'm going to have everything in this pile sorted in less than 15 minutes.This gamifies the experience, making it more of an engaging challenge you want to win.

- If we're talking about your home office space, categories you might have could be writing utensils, paperclips, and items with similar functions like staples, unused paper, notepads, and notes you've written (don't read them now) just put them in the "need to read this and figure out where it goes" pile, books, invoices, etc.

Once you've gotten rid of the biggest things, you'll realize that it looks much better. You have no more garbage there, and all of the things that remain are things that you know you will need or use. This is no longer a pile of unknown things that intimidates you to look at or go through. Instead, you have been able to be intentional about what remains in a very short amount of time.

This systematic method of picking things up and getting them out of the way will make the rest easier to tackle, and getting rid of them first will give you a quick sense of accomplishment at how much of a difference you just made in just a few moves.

A word of advice in your sorting process. Try your best not to have a miscellaneous pile. That's how you got here, to begin with. All of this was essentially filed as miscellaneous or to be dealt with later. We need to sort it out more specifically now so that we can figure out what to do with it. If you only have one or two of this type of item and it really doesn't go with other items or have a home anywhere else that you can think of, consider other aspects of it, such as its function or what actions it applies to. This may help you to better sort it into the existing piles that you have.

Once you've sorted your garbage bags, make sure you get them out of the way. If a bag can go outside, take it there. If it needs to go by the door for now, then bring it there. It's time to focus on the piles you have made. When decluttering with ADHD- it's best to go for the low-hanging fruit first. Because quick wins are more likely to keep you moving, we know that more complicated and time-consuming tasks can shut us right down.

So if you find one of your piles looks easiest to put away or deal with, do that first. With ADHD, one of our biggest barriers to getting organized, aside from lack of consistency, is demotivation. Once we get bored or feel like a task is too hard and we're not getting enough of a reward from it, we quickly give it up. So do your best to keep your motivation up by making this entire process a continuous feed of small successes.

## Keep Going for the Quick Wins

You've sorted out the cluttered area, you got rid of the garbage, donations, and recyclables. Now you know that what remains in the piles are things that need to be put away. If you are working with clothes or another form of textiles, now is when you'll fold them. If there is a pile of things that needs to be hung, you can do that before or after you fold the other piles. Remember - quick wins. If you know a pile needs to get hung. Go hang it up, but do not get stuck in the closet trying to organize it all. Resist that urge because it will slow you down and threatens to derail the whole process. Remind yourself that organizing is a different task. You are still decluttering. So you're not getting sidetracked, and you are prioritizing decluttering at this moment. Because decluttering is less detail-oriented than organizing, we are aiming for speed and continuous movement.

Choose the pile that looks easiest to you. If you are having trouble identifying what to start with, there are a few ways to choose.

- Go for the big things. There are likely fewer of them.
- Go for piles that have the most similar items. These tend to be easier to deal with. The pile of unused notepads, the pile of post-it notes or office supplies, the pile of jeans or t-shirts, the pile of books.
- Go for the things that do have a somewhat established place to go - it doesn't have to be a perfect spot for them - but if you know your top desk drawer holds the pens and office supplies, get them in there.
- Again, resist the urge to organize that drawer perfectly. Speed is the goal here. Slowly enough to not throw things haphazardly, thereby creating more clutter, but that's about it. We're not getting super organized, we are putting things in the vicinity of where they go in a way that's not a disaster. If you can put it away and leave it looking somewhat organized, great. If the organizing aspect will take you more than 2-3 minutes, then keep it moving, and you'll get organized later. We are getting rid of the absolute nonsensical chaos. So it won't be beautiful just yet, but it certainly won't be a mess anymore.

If you have something that literally does not have any home at all. Make one. Even if that home is temporary. How do you choose a quick home for this category?

- Have you been putting this thing in a certain area naturally?
- What type of area makes sense for this thing?
- Does it need to be visible?

- Can it go in a drawer? In a basket? In a section of the desk?
- If you picture this item in others' homes, where does it tend to go?
- Remember, this does not have to be the item's forever home. We are just decluttering and making a space for that category of item. Keep it moving.
- Do not choose a space that requires you to reorganize a different space you are not currently focusing on.
    - For example, if I decide that my unread mail should go in the basket on my kitchen counter - but that basket is currently holding a bunch of other items that are not included in the area that I'm currently decluttering, then I can either dump the basket quickly and decide to go through those things later when I'm done with this section, or the unread mail gets a different temporary home for now. But I don't stop organizing one section midway, just to start another. We need to keep the momentum going.

Now start putting things where they can go. What often holds up the decluttering process or stops it from happening altogether is the fact that we too often try to combine it with organizing. We are not organizing yet, we are just getting rid of the chaos. We will make it beautiful later. The quickest way to overwhelm yourself or take so much time that you cannot complete the task is to confuse organization with decluttering. Focus solely on getting rid of the clutter.

This means our piles are getting dealt with. The items in the piles are going somewhere. Office supplies get put in the drawer if there is room for them. If there is other stuff in there, that's okay. If they still fit, you can put them in there. If they don't fit and you would have to dump the drawer first, consider putting them in a different drawer or spot, and you will address that drawer later. Clothes get hung, linens get put away, jeans, sweatshirts, and unused paper. They all get a home. They each go together with other items from their category.

Once you've done this, that section is decluttered. It should not have taken you very long. An hour at most, but more likely half an hour if you maintain your momentum and keep it to a small space. Decluttering in small spaces like this helps you realize how achievable it is to declutter an area and makes you more likely to commit to decluttering another small area next.

If you were able to declutter a small section in 30 minutes, then pick another spot that day. If you commit 1 hour to decluttering each day, before you know it, you will have decluttered a whole room. Making a series of small achievable commitments helps you to keep making progress. It also addresses one of the major issues surrounding clutter for the person with ADHD, which is feeling overwhelmed to the point of impossibility. In this process, we are showing ourselves that it can be done, it gets done quickly, and it's no big deal.

So the lessons we learned in this section are: commit to small spaces, speed over perfection, remember the distinction between decluttering and organizing, go for quick wins, sort things based on type or function, and be willing to give them temporary homes when their forever home is currently taken or when you haven't figured out where you really want them to go yet. That is totally fine. Decluttering is very much about speed, quick wins, and progress, not perfection. Try to engage a flexible mindset by being willing to try different spaces for different things later on and knowing that the place you choose for it today does not have to be permanent if it ends up ineffective. This takes the pressure off making the right choice and allows you to try different things.

## Your Ongoing System to Stay Decluttered

Staying decluttered relies on something that, quite frankly, we are terrible at - consistency. Research has shown that we don't struggle as much with the strategies of getting things done as we do with the ability to persist (Durand et al., 2020). We tend to let things fall off, as you are well aware.

This is where it's crucial to start implementing some of the habit building strategies that you learned in the previous chapter. Keep in mind that by now you know how to get heavily cluttered areas decluttered. It takes a bit of time, strategy, and rolling up your sleeves to address the piles of chaos, but it can absolutely be done. Beyond that, we know that small areas can be decluttered fairly quickly and that the process can be pretty rewarding along the way. This is meant to reassure you that it is very possible to get back on track if you do have a lapse in consistency like many of us do. As we move forward we'll show you how to catch your slips early.

Don't forget some of the strategies that you have learned to maintain your motivation. And build daily habits. Listen to music to keep your pace up, good options can be upbeat music or workout music playlists. Steer clear of movies or shows which will potentially take your focus away.

Now, to maintain the work you have done, let's assume you do plan to have some consistency around staying decluttered. You'll want to create a habit of running through each room in your house daily. By doing it this way, it will take you less than 10-15 minutes total each day to stay decluttered. Low-traffic areas, such as a bedroom, dining room, laundry room, etc., may only need to be addressed once toward the end of the day.

High-traffic areas should get decluttered twice. Once in the afternoon and again in the evening. While I mention that your entire daily decluttering process should only take 10-15 minutes, that's because each time you are decluttering a room, it is only taking 2-3 minutes at most.

Don't forget that next up is our organization system. So that means that once you are decluttered and fully organized, your daily decluttering will consist of taking 2-3 minutes in both the afternoon and before bed to declutter the living room, kitchen, bathroom, and whatever other areas get high traffic. Each of those spaces gets 2-3 minutes of your time. The low-traffic spaces will get a once-over in the evening before you wrap up your day. These areas should only take 1-2 minutes at most.

What you are doing during this daily decluttering process is looking for anything that you may have left out or absentmindedly put down. You're also scanning for garbage or anything you should have tossed out at that moment. An empty water bottle, a napkin, a sticky note that you started to write on but don't actually need anymore. It's that quick.

How will you remember to do it? You've got two options. You can set yourself a reminder - which may be a good idea in the beginning, regardless. Set the alarm in your phone at times that will work for you, generally in the afternoon and evening, to take a few minutes and scan each room for clutter to get rid of.

These brief moments of decluttering should ideally utilize habit stacking and other strategies that you learned in the previous chapter to start generating some consistency. It's simple enough to choose two times during your day where you can devote 15 minutes or less to decluttering your space. Examples of when this could take place is after you finish work and before you go to bed. Or when you wake up in the morning if you don't want to do it at night. Either way, just twice a day when you can commit a few minutes will go far in keeping the clutter from building up again.

So for your daily decluttering - you might stack your afternoon run-through onto the end of lunch if you work from home. Once you put your plate in the sink - you do a quick run-through of the clutter in the kitchen, then prompting you to run through the other high-traffic areas real quick and just pick up anything you see that is lying around.

If you work outside of the home, I would suggest doing your afternoon run-through close to when you get home. Chances are you might have left a bit of clutter around when you were getting ready to leave in the morning, and walking through the house just to pick these things up is a good way to separate the first half of your day from the second. Once you get home and do a quick declutter that should take you less than 5 minutes, you are ready to transition into your downtime. Then you'll repeat this process at the end of the day, just doing a quick walkthrough of each of your rooms with the intention of being able to wake up to a nice clutter-free space in the morning.

Pro tip - try to do your daily decluttering at the same time or associate with the same regular habits each day - this way, it becomes automatic. Sticking to it daily will prevent you from having to do the declutter deep dive that we did earlier in this chapter.

## How to Recognize When it's Accumulating Again

Have you been decluttering daily? If not, then it's probably accumulating again. Look around and check out your surfaces. Are there things on them that don't live there, even if they seem benign? Then it's starting again. As a general rule, your surfaces should look clear or very well organized. If they do not, this is a sign that your clutter is picking back up. If they do look clear and well organized at the end of each day, and they just get a bit cluttered during the day before you've picked things up, then you are still fine.

## Work with yourself rather than against yourself

Are you realizing that your unread mail is always the outlier? That this is always the type of clutter you find yourself picking up? If you recognize patterns like that, something about that system is not working for you. Don't be afraid to make changes. In fact, this whole book and process is about better learning yourself and what works for you. Don't spend too long fighting it and trying to force systems that don't work for you. You're unlikely to win that battle. You are much better off leaning into it. Think about why that one type of thing is always out. Perhaps the location you chose for it is not the best place for it. Perhaps you need a different habit for addressing that thing altogether. Consider other ways you might address it.

# Less is more

Mind your impulse buys. Your wallet and your newly decluttered space will thank you. People with ADHD tend to buy things more impulsively than those who do not have ADHD. This can result in having a lot of extra things that we really don't need. While fully addressing impulsive spending and shopping is well beyond the scope of this book - I would suggest really asking yourself if you need that thing before you buy it. What will be different in your life if you buy it versus if you don't? Can you wait a day or two to decide whether you really have to have it? If you do buy it, are you able to get rid of something in its place? Applying the one-in, one-out rule. Something comes into the house, something goes out - with the mindset of reducing clutter. Being aware of this behavior and using some of these strategies can help you to accumulate things at a slower pace and ideally avoid building up the same clutter that led to more donations and garbage bags than you thought was even possible.

Additionally, when you have fewer things, your entire space is easier to organize, easier to clean, and easier to maintain.

## Ways to live more minimally

How many dishes do you really need?
When was the last time you used that?
What would the impact on your day-to-day functioning be if you got rid of that?
Is this a "just in case" item?
Is the sentimental value really worth holding onto this item?
Do you frequently look at it or engage with it in some way?

Often we think we need more than we actually need. Clutter doesn't only come from things lying around chaotically, it can also come from having too many of that type of thing. 'Just-in-case' items are most often forgotten about when those 'just in case' moments arise. At one point, I owned 3 tape measures and 2 small toolboxes. You would think I was a handyman. When in fact, I used these things so infrequently that I forgot I had them and mistakenly bought duplicates. I also had bins of things full of just-in-case items under my bed. While I thought I was being organized by having them in bins, the entire storage space under my bed was full of just-in-case bins. That space was later put to much better use by getting rid of the just-in-case stuff and using that area to hold my out-of-season clothes.

So thoroughly consider the things you are holding onto, don't be afraid to let things go, and choose quickly. We are talking about material things here. You will know if you absolutely need something, but if you are in doubt or have to think too long, chances are you really don't need that thing. When it comes to decluttering, we need to keep it moving.

## KEY TAKEAWAYS:

- Clutter is common among people with ADHD and will be a significant barrier to organizing if not dealt with.
- Start with relatively small areas. You want to aim for short periods of intense focus.
- Have 3 bags on hand when you start out - garbage, donation, recycling.
- Create specific piles categories by the type of thing and/or it's function

ADHD ORGANIZATION AND CLEANING

- Sort items quickly and go for quick wins. You want to avoid getting sidetracked and maintain your motivation to keep pushing forward.
- Prioritize decluttering - NOT organizing. One thing at a time. If you accidentally start trying to organize while in the middle of decluttering, there is a good chance that you won't finish either.
- Progress, not perfection.
- Daily decluttering can become a quick and automatic habit
- Less is more - let things go and think before you buy

# Part 2

## Organizing Room by Room

# CHAPTER 5

# Your Simple Organization System – How to Make Organizing Automatic and Easy

Once you've decluttered, you're ready to start getting organized. Despite the fact that ADHD symptoms lend themselves to creating disorganization and chaos, we tend to do much better when surrounded by organized spaces that feel more calm and under control. So this is what we want to create for ourselves and our loved ones if we live with them. We want the home that we live in to be a calm, serene, and functional space where we can get what we need and feel proud of the home that we live in.

There are two aspects to consider when developing your organization system. One is getting organized from a place of being disorganized. The second is maintaining organization with an ongoing system.

# What do we mean by organizing?

We mean arranging the items that are contained in your house so that their location makes more sense and is more useful to you and your household. Typically, this involves putting similar items together, making them accessible to you if they are regularly used, or storing them so that they are out of the way, but you can easily find and retrieve them later.

As you choose where items will go, you'll consider not only the type of item that it is, but also its function. For example, if I have a cookbook. Yes, it's a book. But it makes much less sense to put it in your home office or living room, versus finding a place for it to stay in the kitchen.

Ultimately, you'll want items to be in the room they belong in, ideally stored with other similar items, and you'll want to consider whether the area you put them in is efficient, accessible, and aesthetically pleasing.

As you consider this view of organization, you can start to get a sense of why decluttering was such an important prerequisite. People with ADHD often have a lot of extra things that we often don't need. Additionally, those things can sometimes land in the wrong rooms altogether. Upon completing the decluttering phase, you likely got rid of a lot of excess, leaving you with only the essentials, the things that have significant meaning to you, and deserve to have an intentional spot in your home.

# Bringing back the basics

As we proceed with organizing - we need to bear in mind the skills that you have previously learned.

## Small Achievable Steps

Breaking things down helps to address both procrastination and de-motivation by reducing the potential to feel overwhelmed and reducing the level of commitment required. It also helps as you work toward building habits by starting with small tasks and gradually adding to them as they become easier and more automatic.

## Time Blocks

Small intentional time blocks make a task feel less daunting because you're committing to the time you set rather than the entire task. These time blocks can be put into your daily planner or calendar. For example if you feel overwhelmed at the idea of going through the mail on your counter, you can commit to just 10 minutes. Set a timer and then the expectation is no longer about completing the mail, but about giving it 10 minutes of focused attention. You've now cracked through your avoidance and made a dent in the task. Upon finishing the 10 minutes, you can decide when to come back for the next 10.

## Remember Your Why

Your 'Why' is the reason you picked up this book and what you stand to gain if you are successful in your home organizing endeavors. You may also have smaller 'whys' that pertain to each room. Having a clean and organized kitchen as we discussed in Chapter 3 can contribute to your sense of control and confidence at the beginning of your day. While having an organized bedroom space can provide you with a peaceful sanctuary at the end of the day or a place to connect with your partner away from the rest of the world. What matters most is that it feels important to you and provides the foundational incentive you need to take steps forward.

## Include Rewards Throughout the Process

Incorporating rewards prior to, during, and after tasks can boost your dopamine and your ability to complete tasks. If I want to feel more confident in my work life and improve my productivity, I may realize the importance of having an organized home office - my 'why'. So I set goals to get organized and stay organized. I break down the tasks involved and I work on them while doing things I enjoy like listening to playlists or TedTalks. I check the task off my list each time I accomplish it and I add $20 to a fund for each week that I don't miss a day. This reward goes toward a new design software I've been wanting to splurge on.

## Make the Time

We don't find extra time to organize our homes, we need to be intentional about making the time because we establish that having a clean and organized home is a priority. Putting the time into your calendar makes you more likely to accomplish the tasks you set out to do, rather than vaguely expecting that you'll do it at some point in the day. This leaves much less possibility for procrastination, time blindness, and poor working memory to get in the way.

## Use Tools and Resources

We have thoroughly explored the various tools and resources at your disposal that will make cleaning and organizing more feasible as they will help to address some of the additional needs we might experience with ADHD. Once you establish clear plans for how to use each of these resources as part of your organization system, you no longer need to worry about forgetfulness, working memory issues, and time blindness as you actively change and reward your new daily habits.

## Getting organized

Get a label maker. This helps in a few ways. First, you'll be able to find the things you are looking for more easily. Second, it can make you more likely to put the item back in that place and to not let other things that don't belong go in there. It's like a little added nudge against getting disorganized again.

If that drawer says "office supplies," you'll have a quick reminder that you are deliberately working against yourself if you put something else in there. This helps to address your impulsivity at that moment. It's impulsivity that says, "who cares? I just want it out of the way." That's how doom piles get formed. Seeing that label makes you second guess that impulsive decision for just a moment so that you can recognize what you are doing and think, "Okay, it doesn't actually go there.

One of the antidotes to impulsive behavior is consequential thinking. This means assessing the potential consequences of your impulsive decision before you go through with it. When we deliberately and impulsively choose to put something in a space that is clearly not labeled for that thing and is, in fact, labeled for something else, we are very quickly reminding ourselves that we may forget where this thing is in the future. We are also forced to recognize that we are choosing to be disorganized at this moment which could be the first step or one of many steps on our way back to chaos. That split second of consequential thinking could be the helpful nudge that pushes us back in the right direction. When it comes to ADHD, we may need lots of those nudges.

## Storage Tips

Now that you have decluttered, do you actually have enough storage space? This is when we start to carefully consider whether we need additional storage shelves, bins, baskets, etc. But do not buy them without having a sense of what will go in them and where they will go. You'll consider this more closely as you work on bringing organization to the chaos. See our previous section on impulsive buying. If your purchases, even for organizational purposes, are not well thought out, you could inadvertently be adding to your clutter.

As a kid, I LOVED getting the backpack that had the most storage pockets. I was obsessed with all of those storage pockets and all the potential they had. But I fully lacked organization skills or any sort of system. And every year, no matter how many cool storage areas my backpack had - everything would end up shoved in random places in the most ineffective, inefficient way possible. You don't want that to happen with all the poorly planned storage bings you could impulsively buy. Getting bins or containers, with no plan or system in place for those exact bins or containers, will only add to the problem.

# Putting it All into Action

## Step 1: Build Your Roadmap

Here is where we create the plan. We'll use the example of your living room, as it is important to start with the areas you spend the most time in. You want to avoid going in haphazardly and instead start organizing in an order that has some strategy and intention behind it. This doesn't mean it needs to be perfect or that it can't be adjusted.

But ultimately, you want to approach all of your rooms in a way that feels as manageable as possible. Creating a plan or roadmap helps you do that.

Grab a piece of paper and a pen. Go to your living room and stand in the center so that you can get a good visual of what every area looks like, including getting a good assessment of its current state. You're going to be writing a list of the areas in your living room in a particular order. As you get to areas that require more work, you'll also be jotting down some notes about those spots.

As you look at your living room, start by identifying the areas that look the best. These are the areas that don't really need rearranging or reorganizing, rather, they just need to be straightened up. Say you have a bookshelf, and you're happy with where your bookshelf is in the living room. It's mostly filled with books and maybe random papers. But overall, it looks pretty good. If this is the spot in the room that looks to be the most organized, put it at the top of the list. You're going to list the areas in your living room, starting with the spots that need the least work, and moving down to the spots that need the most work.

If your living room feels so chaotic that you can't even begin to make sense of individual areas in the way I've mentioned above, then picture your living room as a big clock. Straight ahead of you is 12, a bit to the right of that is 1, directly to your right is 3, behind you is 6, and so on. You can break it up into 12 small sections like this. If you can notice any 'hours' of the clock that seem like they would be the easiest and quickest to address, then list those first, moving along your list down toward the areas that need the most work.

If you feel there is really no way to discern better condition from worse condition in your living room. Then you'll simply start at 12 and work your way around. That will be the order that you complete sections in your living room. However, make sure that if you are at this stage and ready to organize, you have decluttered first. If you skip over decluttering and jump straight to organizing, you'll likely run into problems. Remember, we got rid of a lot of excess in the declut tering phase so that we could effectively organize now.

Now let's run through the list quickly. You have sections of your living room listed - either by name (bookshelf, couch, mantle, coffee table, etc.) or by hour on the clock. This list is quick, and it demonstrates that once you have gotten rid of the clutter, the remaining areas in the room are quite manageable. It also means you can check it off as you make progress, and if you break it up over the course of a few days, you can pick right back up where you left off.

Go through the following steps for each location on your roadmap. Once you're done, each room should be fully organized.

## Step 2: Determine What to Keep in the Room

Things that make sense to stay in a room are the things that will be used in that room. Start with the first area on your roadmap. Now, as you approach areas that need more work and are a bit messier, there are a few questions to ask yourself:

- Does having this piece of furniture here make sense?
  - o If no, move it to the area where it would make more sense before going to the next question
  - o If yes, continue to the next question

- Do the objects in or on this piece of furniture belong in this room?
  - If no, move it/them to a bin for now so that you can bring them to the right room later
  - If yes:
    - Move on to step 3

## Step 3: Pick a Spot that Makes Sense

If the items make sense where they are, then move on to step 4.

If not, then consider the following when deciding where they should go:

Consider the type of item and function

You'll usually want to keep similar items together, but you'll also need to consider how they are used. A cookbook is a good example. You'd generally want to keep your books together on a shelf that's not likely in the kitchen. More likely a bookshelf in the living room, home office, or even bedroom. But a cookbook would more likely be stored in the kitchen if we consider when and how it is used. For another example, coffee beans and sugar are often pantry items. Yet if they are used daily when you make coffee, you might store them closer to the coffee machine.

Choose locations and storage methods with care and purpose

Think about how that item will be used. Envision yourself, or if anyone else lives with you, envision how they or you might go to get that item. If you are putting away the salt and pepper in your kitchen, don't put it on the back of the shelf on the highest shelf of the cabinet. Consider what the moment looks like when you might reach for it -

keep it within easy reach of the stove and likely toward the front of that shelf or cabinet. If you only use the slow cooker once a month, it can probably go in a cabinet to be pulled out when you need it rather than sitting on the counter next to your toaster.

In your process of getting organized, you will likely find items that don't belong in that section. This is another area that can pose a risk of getting sidetracked. Have on a hand a bin/basket/container where you can keep items that go somewhere else. As you are going through this section, you are only keeping items here that should be here. If you are finding things that need to be tossed, they get tossed. If you find items that need to go in a different room or a completely different section of this room, they just go in this bin. To be dealt with after this section is done and possibly in another time block that you have set aside to address the things in this bin.

Now that you've deliberately chosen where everything should go and you're satisfied that those locations make sense, you're ready to move on to step 4.

## Step 4: Arrange in a Way That Works for That Space

Once you've decided where items belong, you'll need to arrange them. Consider the following:

How often does this item get used?

My planner sits in front of a kitchen organizer on my counter. It typically sits there open to the week we are on because I refer to it and may write in multiple times per day. My checkbook gets used much less often. It sits in a drawer of that same kitchen organizer. It's important and can't be lost, but I generally use it once a month so it can stay in the drawer. The same goes for your travel mugs - if they don't get used often, they don't need to be up front with your daily cups and mugs. Instead, they can go toward the back of that cabinet.

This rule applies to clothing as well. If jeans are not your favorite thing to wear and you prefer sweatpants, the sweatpants need to be more visible and more easily accessible than the jeans. Your organization system needs to be individualized and cater to your lifestyle and your individual preferences while also making sense for the space and storage of the items themselves.

Displaying and Storing Items

Wherever possible, store items neatly and away unless they are used every day for most of the day or unless they make sense to display, like books, DVDs, or collections that are meant for display. The fewer things you have out, the more spacious and organized your living room will feel. Consider placing appropriately sized baskets on shelves so that the shelves are still easy on the eyes while being able to still hold everything you want.

Items tend to look better, and spaces look cleaner when things are in an order that makes sense. For example, the books in my living room. They are children's books, and they are arranged according to size. Biggest to smallest. It's pleasing to the eye. The bookshelf in my room with my own books on it is arranged according to the genre. These are both sets of books, but they serve different audiences, and the way they are currently arranged suits the person who is looking through them. This makes them more accessible and efficient. Both sets of books also look clean and neat in how they are set up.

As you follow your roadmap, repeating these steps for each area in the room, you'll fall into a rhythm where the tasks start to flow from one to the next. Before you know it, you'll be standing in an organized room that you can feel proud of.

## Stay on Task and Don't Let Perfectionism Derail You

Where ADHD is concerned, our tendency toward perfectionism more often results in not getting the job done because we spent all of our energy and motivation arranging our shirts by color or getting our Tupperware drawer to look like the one we saw on Pinterest. If you want to do these kinds of "extras" after you've gotten organized, have at it. But our task at the moment is getting organized. Arranging things in a way that is efficient, accessible, and looks nice, not looks 'perfect.'

Along with time blocking and breaking the task down into bite-size pieces - make sure you choose a time of day that works for you. You may be more of a night owl. Or you may find that your energy burst only comes mid-day while you are at work, meaning that weekends may be more important for your organizing plans. Ultimately, you may need to experiment with different times of day for this. Don't expect to get organized in one day. You'll likely be doing this process over several days and possibly a few weeks, depending on the time you can set aside for it. How long it takes will also depend on the size of your home and the number of things that need to be organized. Don't let this deter you. This process is achievable for anyone who follows the guidelines and suggestions. You also have practical strategies that directly address *how* you can follow through on the suggestions without your symptoms derailing you. This book allows you to create plans and systems that are individualized so that you can do what works for you, your home, and your lifestyle.

It's all about addressing our biggest issues which include procrastination, motivation, focus, and seeing tasks through to completion. By making the individual goals small, making the process rewarding, and setting your sights on one small task at a time with minimal allowance for distractions or sidetracking, you will steadily chip away at the organization project that is your home.

One of the methods I prefer to use involves tiny bursts of productivity spread across my day. So I'll take half an hour in the morning, I may take another half an hour mid-day, and another in the evening. These small bursts of time and focus are much more powerful for me than if I tried to commit to an hour or two of organizing. That often feels daunting and overwhelming to someone with ADHD, especially since time blindness can make that level of time commitment to a task that you already did not want to do feel like forever.

So again, experiment with the times. Set reasonable expectations where you understand that the entire process of getting your home from a state of chaos into a state or organization can take a few weeks. Know that the exact amount of time it takes will vary depending on their homes, items, behaviors, and choices throughout this process. I can assure you that if you stick to the strategies outlined in this book, you will have success, and you will have the skills you need to sustain your results.

## Maintaining Organization

Just as things in your home can often get cluttered easily, they can also get disorganized easily. Whereas your decluttering plan involves tiny daily moments of decluttering, I also recommend 15 minutes of daily organizing and once-weekly organization upkeep of about an hour. The hour-long session could be adjusted depending on the size and needs of your house.

The idea is that once you are organized, it should only take a couple of min per room to stay organized. A book on the shelf may get out of place, the spices in your kitchen may have been taken down while cooking, and you can put them back up on the rack. Each room should take no more than a couple of minutes at most. You also reserve an hour at one point each week to run through each room, doing a deeper organization as needed for your situation.

This means that during your quicker run through you're not worried about making it perfect, but you still maintain an organized feel in your house while knowing you can perfect it during that longer session if needed. Maybe your spices went back in the cabinet or on the rack when you quickly got them off the counter earlier in the week, but now you want to arrange them so they look better. Perhaps you had an event to go through, and you went through a bunch of clothes figuring out what to wear. In your 15 minutes, you got everything back up on the hangers and put it back in the closet, but you still want to fix up where you put everything. This weekly deeper organizing session is really taking the time to re-set exactly where you want things to go.

As you create your organization system, don't forget to accommodate yourself. In addition to the dirty laundry hamper in my bedroom, I also have a clean laundry basket. These baskets are from the same set, slightly different heights and shapes, but they have the same aesthetic, they go with the bedroom, and they are both super important and intentional. Just as I wouldn't leave my dirty laundry to lay around anywhere and I leave it in the hamper until I get a moment to put it in the washing machine, I also acknowledge that I am not always able to fold my laundry as soon as it is done drying. Although I believe it is good practice to do so, I know myself and my lifestyle, and it just does not happen this way. So I have a clean laundry basket. This stops the laundry from piling up on a chair or on my bed, or on top of a dresser. It goes into its designated spot until I fold it. Now if I have time or make time to do it during the week, it gets done, but if I don't and I get all the way up to my organization upkeep day - then that is when it gets folded.

So, your hour devoted to organization each week is when you go through that clean laundry that you still haven't put away and get it put away; you fix the books if they got disorganized and left in different parts of the living room, and you address anything that is left in the 'to be addressed' paper basket in your kitchen or wherever you keep it. Those papers that need to be tended through get looked at least once on the weekends so that you can address them or decide that they need to wait till the following week, but either way, they get looked at, and a decision is made about what to do with them.

So between decluttering and organizing, that's a max of 30 minutes daily and an hour on one chosen day each week. Just to put that in perspective, that's less than the time it would take for you to watch one show or movie on Netflix each day. It's closer to listening to 10 or fewer songs. And your 'long' period of organization that occurs weekly is about as long as one show, and that's only happening once per week.

If you're someone who spends time on social media and this time commitment to organizing feels daunting, try to change your perspective on it. Imagine you could only use social media for 30 minutes per day and an hour on the weekends. Does it still feel like a lot of time? This is not to shame you at all. This example is to demonstrate how our perception and our dopamine reward response can play such a huge role.

You've already learned some specific tips on increasing motivation, rewarding yourself, and beating procrastination - so if those things come back around and threaten to make your goal of getting organized seem impossible, I urge you to revisit those chapters. Once you understand what your needs are and how your brain works, you absolutely can achieve your goals.

The time when you are getting organized is super important to stay on top of your symptoms. Try to make sure you are enjoying this time - by playing music, audiobooks, etc., sipping a latte, and stepping back every 15 min or so to admire your progress. Keep moving fairly quickly. Setting milestones for yourself can help with this. I'll be done going through this drawer in 10 minutes. This particular piece of the task will be completed at this time. Little milestones like this can also gamify the experience a bit which can be naturally rewarding, especially for people with ADHD.

# Assess and reassess your storage strategies

Once you have gotten things organized is when you will have the opportunity to determine if particular strategies are working for you. Remember, we want to create habits that are easy for you to maintain.

Does it work that you keep jackets in the coat closet? It may look 10x neater that way, and it's easy to tell why you put it there, but if in the day-to-day that results in you not wanting to take the time to open the closet door and put the jacket on a hanger, so instead you just throw it on the couch or on your bed, then you may need to re-assess that strategy. An over-the-door coat hook may be more beneficial for your daily jacket because you're simply more likely to use it.

The systems that work are not necessarily the ones that look the best or make the most sense. The systems that work are the ones that you'll use. Yes, we want them to be more efficient than the chaos, and we want your new system to look better than the chaos. But remember that they are literally no good if you don't use them. So if something is not working after a few weeks of trying to do it according to your original setup, then it is time to try a different system.

# Key Takeaways

Have a step-by-step plan:

- Step 1. Build You Roadmap
  - For each room, list the areas you'll be going through from most to least organized
  - If this type of breakdown doesn't work for that room, than picture it like a clock and break it down into 12 small sections

- o You'll use this list to keep track and check things off as you go
- Step 2. Determine What to Keep in the Room
  - o Start with the first area on your list
  - o Follow the steps from here down through step 4, then come back up to this step for the next area and so on.
  - o Does the furniture make sense where it is? If not, you'll need to move it.
  - o Do the items belong in this room?
    - ▪ If not, place them in a bin to be moved to the room they go in later, then move forward to the next step
    - ▪ If so, continue to step 3.
- Step 3. Pick a Spot that Makes Sense
  - o If the items there make sense in that spot, and just need better arranging, proceed to step 4
  - o If you're not yet sure where they should go:
    - ▪ Consider the types of items, as you'll group similar items together
    - ▪ Consider how you use them
- Step 4. Arrange Items in a Way that Works for that Space
  - o Consider how often you use the item
  - o Similar items look better together
  - o Arrange neatly and out of sight where possible
- Make sure you declutter before attempting to organize
- These chapters build upon one another. Keep in mind what you have learned in previous chapters
- Organize one room and one small section at a time
- Start with the high-traffic rooms first

- Labeling, storage containers and organizers, and careful choice of where you store things will come in handy
- Individualize room plans to meet your needs, preferences, and lifestyle
- Use the skills you've learned to curb perfectionism, procrastination, and low motivation
- Maintaining means
  - Decluttering for a max of 30 min per day broken into two 15-minute blocks. It will likely go faster.
  - Reorganizing for one hour per week, this time will also likely go faster.
- Assess your storage areas and be willing to change them to find what works best for you in the long run

## CHAPTER 6

# The Living Room

Your living room is likely the most high traffic room in your house. Because you spend most of your time here and any guests you have would undoubtedly spend most of their time here as well, this is where we'll start. Once you see that you can tackle the most frequently used room in the house, you'll start to get a sense of just how achievable getting and staying organized really is.

Although everyone's living room space can differ, you likely have some of the following areas:

- Seating areas, including couches, chairs, and ottomans
- Coffee table and End tables
- TV stand
- Book shelf
- Display shelves or mantel
- Additional storage cabinets or shelving

## Seating Areas

There are endless ways to arrange the furniture in a living room, but ultimately you want it to be intentional. If the focal point of your living room is the TV, then couches and chairs are oriented toward that. Seating areas should be conducive to a conversation between people seated in different spots. Furniture shouldn't be cluttered and awkward to move around. The seating that you have in the room is useful, and if it is more of a display piece, make sure it's not just creating another surface to collect clutter.

Too many decorative pillows on couches and chairs can get disorganized quickly. If you have throw blankets, these can be arranged neatly on a couch or chair. If they have a tendency to look messy, keep them in a storage ottoman, nearby drawer, or basket.

## Coffee Table / End Tables

Ideally, there should be at least one table surface within reach of every seating option so that people have a place to put things down while in that space. But bear in mind these surfaces can be clutter magnets. Make a point to leave these spaces open. You might have one decorative item in the middle of your coffee table. You might have a lamp on an end table.

These areas are meant to be useful while you are in the living room if you need to put down a book, laptop, or drink. Outside of being used at that moment, they should be clear. This makes the room look more open and organized.

## TV Stand

This is where your consoles will go. Refrain from putting decorative items around the TV or on the TV stand. This makes the area look cluttered and messy. Try to keep wires out of sight or neatly tied together. Whether you keep the remote controls here is a personal preference. You might opt to keep them on the TV stand when the living room is not in use, or you might keep them in a drawer of the coffee table or end table since you typically watch TV when seated on a couch or chair.

Any drawers or cabinets in your TV stand should contain things like videos, DVDs, and games for the consoles you have. If you have a TV stand with lots of extra storage space, this is where you might keep other items that are relevant to the living room, such as books or board games. If you have large shelves on your TV stand - choose simple-looking baskets to hold your items. This will look more organized than placing things directly on the shelf.

## Shelving

If you are using a shelf for books, only have books on that shelf. Don't mix books with other items. This can look messy and disorganized. Arrange the books in a way that makes sense for you. This might be by genre, by author, or alphabetically. Choose one way that makes sense and stick to that so that you always know where to find the book you need and where to put it back.

Display shelves are often used in living rooms to hold pictures or other sentimental or decorative items. Be intentional about the items you place on these shelves. Too many things, too close together, will look chaotic. Choose a few times, and space them out. Try to have similar items on the shelf. Whether it's pictures, trophies, or figurines, the shelf should look cohesive rather than a mashup of random items.

For additional storage shelves, keep their size of them in mind. Whenever possible, use a bin, basket, or some type of organizer. Otherwise, the shelf is likely to quickly gather random items. Use labels ff you have a lot of storage shelving in your living room. This will make it more likely that you know where things are and that you put them back in their place. It will also make your organization maintenance quicker.

## Pro Tip for the Living Room

Because this is a high-traffic area used in many different ways, it can easily get messy and cluttered. Consider having one basket, bin, or drawer that is a small catchall area. This acts as your backup. If you are in a moment where you don't have time to put something where it goes, you can put it in this basket. It's better than leaving it on the couch or coffee table. It will then become part of your normal routine to check and address the things in that basket daily or weekly, depending on how quickly things might accumulate in it.

If a room looks messy already, we are more likely to leave things lying around. But if a room appears to be neat and tidy, it's more obvious to us when we go to leave something out. This basket helps keep the room looking neat and organized while still acknowledging that you might not always have the time to put it where it goes.

## CHAPTER 7
# The Bathroom

Your bathroom is likely much smaller than your living room and is typically made up of sections that are easier to define and generalize.

- the closet, if you have one
- additional cabinets or shelving
- linen tower
- medicine cabinet
- storage areas beneath your sink which can include drawers
- inside the shower/bath area
- countertops

Primary strategies that you'll want to remember in the bathroom are that you want to limit the appearance of clutter in this small space and you also want to group like items together.

## Countertop

Consider what items really need to be on your countertop. At a minimum, you should have soap and a hand towel. Anything else is a personal choice. Bathroom organizer sets are typically a nice way to store the items that go on your countertop. This could also include toothbrushes, toothpaste, hand lotion, and tissues.

If you have a large bathroom countertop, you can probably have these things out in their organizers and still have space to spare so that it doesn't look too cluttered. If you have a smaller countertop in your bathroom, you'll want to stick to the soap and hand towel and keep your other items stored out of view.

## Closets, Linen Tower, and Cabinets

The linen tower or closet should be used to hold your towels, bathmats, hand towels, and bathrobe if you use one. If you have more space in there, this is also a good spot for extra toilet paper and tissues. If you have even more room, you can store backup shampoos, conditioners, soaps, shower gels, etc. Again, this is where your individual preference comes into play.

Underneath the bathroom sink and among the drawers will also depend on your personal preference. You'll likely be storing additional cleaning supplies, possibly larger items like hair dryers, straighteners, electric razors, brushes, etc.

Ultimately the way you use this space is completely based on your personal preference - but keep similar items together and consider how often and when you use the items. This will better inform where you choose to place which items. The same goes for additional cabinet space. It comes down to what items you have, whether you feel you need to keep those items or if they are never used, and how often and in what context you use those items.

## Shower/Bath Area

The shower or bath area definitely benefits from an organizer. Get one that you like the look of, and that will stay up on the wall. Many of them can slide down if they don't hang on the shower head, and that will quickly lead to more disorganization.

If your shower has built-in shelves, those are usually not large enough to accommodate everything neatly. So find an organizer that you like, and if possible, check reviews to make sure it stays up. Here is where you'll store conditioner, shampoo, soap, razors, moisturizers, hair masks, body scrubs, loofahs, and anything else related to your shower or bath routine.

## Pro Tips for Organizing the Bathroom

### You'll need smaller organizer bins and/or drawer organizers

There tend to be a lot of smaller items that can gather in the bathroom. If you have large cabinet spaces or large shelves, the bathroom is typically a place where you will benefit from smaller organizers to put on those shelves, in the cabinets, or in the drawers. Even if you don't have incredibly large spaces under your sink or in the cabinet/closet area, it's still very likely that you'll need some smaller organizers to group like items together and to keep them from becoming a doom pile.

## Get Out the Label Maker

With the organizers that you purchased, it makes sense to label them. If you store makeup, you'll want to group it by area of the face and potentially even more categories depending on your collection. These things get labeled clearly. Over-the-counter pain relievers, allergy medicines, first aid – these things get labeled as well. You'll also want to clearly separate cleaning supplies from any products that you'll use on your body. Depending on what goes in your bathroom and the space you have, it is very likely that labels will be helpful here.

## Have Smaller Jars and Bottles Available

Have you ever had a large bottle of conditioner sitting in your bathroom for over a week with less than a quarter of the original contents still in it? It's still more than enough to use a few times, but it can become annoying when you have a large, mostly empty bottle taking up space. They always fall over much easier too. This is where small reusable jars or bottles come in. Use these as soon as your products start getting low to keep things neater. And again, label them.

## Take the Time You Need to Do it Right

The bathroom is another area of your home that you are likely to frequent several times per day. It's also an area that can easily start to look cluttered due to its small size, and it can easily be embarrassing if it looks messy to guests. Depending on the amount of items in your bathroom and the level or organization you still need to do with all of the small things, this room may take you anywhere from 1-3 sessions, which you might decide to spread across a few days. That is totally okay. It's not about speed, it's about getting it done in a way that can be maintained. Quick fixes might look nice at first glance, but they often don't get maintained due to the lack of intention and consideration of where things are placed. Putting in that extra consideration really goes a long way to creating an organization system that you can maintain in the long term.

# CHAPTER 8
# The Kitchen

The kitchen is another main hub of every home. It gets traffic from the beginning to the end of the day and is often frequented by guests as well. Your kitchen is one of the rooms that require the most structure, considering the frequency of use and the way that it needs to function.

Kitchens can also have a lot of variation in how they are laid out, but ultimately we all tend to have similar areas despite the difference in layout, size, shape, etc. You likely have an area where you cook and prepare food, areas to store foods that need to be kept cold and areas where you can store food at room temp. You likely have a sink, dishwasher, or both, and countertops connecting or nearby to all of these things. Some kitchens have enough space for a table, breakfast bar, or both.

- Pantry
- Cabinets
- Countertops/Island
- Table/Breakfast bar

- Refrigerator
- Sink/Dishwasher
- Trash/Recycles

## Pantry

If you have a separate pantry in addition to your existing cabinet space, this is where you'll keep:

- Canned goods
- Cereals
- Snacks
- Various baking/cooking ingredients

Pantry organizers are a good idea to reduce the clutter of packaging that your goods come in - especially when this package stops you from seeing how much is actually left in the box or bag. This type of packaging can become a major waste of space and make the entire pantry look and feel messier.

Get out your label maker because you'll be taking things out of their bulky packaging to place things in more uniform containers that make finding things a breeze

Try to choose containers that are both transparent and stackable. Often pantry shelves can be tall, but you'll realize that most items don't use that height, so stackable organizers can make the most of this small space. Lazy Susans can also be great for similar items like oils, baking ingredients, or spices.

Before you start organizing this space, make sure that you've already gotten rid of anything that is past the expiration date. Sometimes it can be easy to miss these - just do a quick check as you go through the items you intend to keep in the pantry.

If you are short on space in your pantry, look for door organizers, hooks, and wall dispensers to add additional storage. Organize areas in your pantry by how the things will be used. You can have an area for baking, dinners, snacks, quick lunches, breakfast foods, canned goods, spices, condiments, etc.

## Cabinets

When it comes to organizing your cabinets, it's important to consider whether you have a separate pantry like what is described above or if you are using cabinet space to hold everything. Typically things like canned goods, cereals, snacks, extra paper towels, garbage bags, etc. would go in the pantry, but if you have no pantry, these things are being organized within your cabinet space.

First off, when considering what will go into which cabinets, you'll first consider the location of the cabinets. For example, cabinets near the stove or your food-prepping area will likely contain the items you need for cooking and food prep. Items such as oil, spices, colanders, pots, pans, cutting boards, Tupperware, etc.

While cabinets near the sink area will hold your dishes and glassware. The cabinets underneath the sink typically store cleaning supplies, extra soap, and garbage bags if you don't have a pantry. Consider how you use the items in your kitchen and keep them in the areas that are closest to where they'll be needed or used.

In the absence of a pantry, store food together and organize it by size and type. Similar to the breakdown of areas described in the pantry section, you can do the same with your kitchen cabinets. Areas for breakfast pantry items, dinner pantry items, snacks, condiments, spices, etc. Keep similar items together and taller items toward the back. Keep very large cans or jugs in your bottom cabinets, while smaller items will go toward the front.

As described in the pantry section, clear containers work best to avoid bulky packaging, and labels can be your best friend.

## Countertops

Countertops are often magnets for paperwork doom piles. Try to be intentional with the items on your counter. This will keep the room looking more open and organized as well as more functional.

Some things that will likely stay on your countertops are your small appliances, such as your coffee maker, toaster oven, and your blender - if you use them daily. If you only use it sparingly, this is something that should be stored in a cabinet. The same goes for your slow cooker, food processor, etc. If they are not used frequently, put them away.

While your paperwork should be kept in a spot that makes sense for you, many people often use the countertop as a quick drop spot for mail or other household paperwork that needs to be dealt with. This can result in a paperwork doom pile. If your paperwork doom pile is on the kitchen countertop or anywhere else in the house, you'll want to break it into at least 3 clear categories.

- To pay
- To review/fill out
- To file

If there are other categories that you frequently use, such as coupons or scheduled activities to attend, that need to be put in your calendar, then add those categories. Don't overcomplicate it, but make sure that you've addressed the main areas that typically make up your paperwork clutter. When mail comes in, you'll quickly toss it into one of these baskets or files, and then it will be addressed at least weekly in your organizing routine.

## Table

The table is only useful if it's clear of clutter. Get into the habit of leaving the table clear. Nothing gets stored here aside from a centerpiece if you like and possibly placemats if you want to leave them on the table and ready. Things like napkins or salt/pepper can come out when needed.

## Refrigerator

Chances are, you already know what goes in the fridge and freezer. But the trick can be organizing them so that things are easy to find and don't look like chaos when you open the fridge. This is another place where clear uniform containers come in handy. First off, if you have those drawers at the bottom of your fridge, they're typically meant for your produce. If they have vents, you can slide the vents more open or more closed depending on what you put inside. If you don't have vents, they are just meant to be high-humidity drawers.

Things that go in high-humidity drawers are typically your leafy green vegetables and herbs - things that have the potential to wilt when they dry out. These drawers keep them fresher longer - but don't forget, with ADHD, you might struggle with things being out of sight, out of mind. So pop a label over these drawers to remember what's in there. Low humidity works best for your fruits and just means you leave the vents open to allow the airflow.

Chances are, not all of your produce fits in these drawers, so having clear containers to better sort items and keep them from rolling into each other will help keep the fridge organized. When possible, get rid of extra packaging, just like with your cabinet items.

## Sink/Dishwasher

This section is more about what goes around these areas. If you have a dish rack for dishes that are drying, use it, but try not to let this just become a space where your dishes live all the time. From the dish rack to your meal, back to the sink and dish rack. Make a plan in your organizing routine for when you will empty the dishrack and dishwasher to put those items away.

I have decided not to have a dish rack for this reason. I have a dishwasher, and for anything else that gets hand-washed, I use a hand towel to dry it right away. Otherwise, my dishrack becomes a permanent home for my dishes. Again, it's about knowing yourself.

Having a sponge holder in your sink gives you a place to leave the sponge that's not out on the counter or lost somewhere in the sink. Keeping the dishwasher pods or the dish soap right under the sink keeps your counters neat while keeping what you need close by.

## Trash/Recycles

Trash is pretty straightforward, Keep it in the bin and have a routine for when it gets taken out. If you find it doesn't get taken out frequently enough, get a smaller bin. If you find your bin is too small, consider a slightly larger one while still staying within the realm of normal kitchen bin size.

Have a recycle bin or basket nearby. If you separate your recycles, your bins should also account for this. Recycle bins can usually be smaller and still do the job. If you don't want a bin, you might be fine with a recycle bag. I've seen clients be successful with a dedicated bag that hangs on the bag of the island to keep used water bottles. I personally have a small bag that hangs on the backdoor because that door is situated right between my kitchen and where the bins are outside. So it's easy to grab and move it right out the door.

## Key Takeaways

- Clear uniform containers and labels are best for avoiding clutter in the pantry, cabinets, and refrigerator.
- Get rid of unnecessary bulky packaging.
- Keep everything closest to where you'll use it.
- If you notice any doom piles like paper/mail, get a dedicated mail organizer, thin baskets, or paper organizers and label them.
- Keep trash and recycle bins near eachother and in a spot that's easy to take out.

# CHAPTER 9
# The Bedroom

Bedrooms are another space that can be entirely unique to each individual but for the most part we can assume to include certain things. Like clothes, shoes, a bed, etc. The main areas to consider when organizing your bedroom are:

- The Bed & Under The Bed
- Closet
- Dresser(s)
- Night Tables

## The Bed Area

The only things on top of the bed should be your sheets, blankets, and pillows. If you have space under your bed, this can be a great storage area. You can get storage bins and bags of almost any height to fit under your bed. If you have a smaller living space that doesn't have ample storage, don't let this space go to waste. Use this space for the things that you don't need on a regular basis, like your summer or winter clothes and shoes.

## Closet

The closet is usually the biggest challenge in the bedroom. For someone with ADHD, this often ends up becoming a problematic catchall space. But since you've already decluttered, you've got the hardest part out of the way.

To organize your closet in the best way possible, you'll want to consider the various items that need to be organized. You'll also need to consider whether your current closet setup has the kind of organization space you need. For example, big open spaces can often benefit from adding some additional shelving. But don't go overboard in buying additional organizing units until you see how everything fits.

In general, you'll need to organize:

- Clothes
- Shoes
- Accessories

### Clothes

Break down your clothes into categories. Coats or dresses will get hung on higher racks, while shirts and pants can get hung on mid-level or lower racks. If you have a closet with only one rack, keep the coats furthest toward the back, then dresses, then shirts, then pants closest toward the front. This order works so that you can still see everything. If you have a smaller closet, don't worry about hanging everything. At bare minimum, you'll just want to hang materials that can easily become wrinkled. If you have a bit more space, you'll generally hang any pants, dresses, jackets, and shirts - depending on whether they're likely to wrinkle. Materials that are likely to get stretched out or deformed when hanging should be folded.

T-shirts and Jeans can go either way, and this will depend on what kind of space you have. If you have a small dresser but ample hanging space, you might hang your jeans, but if you only have a small area for hanging and you have a lot more space for folded items, then these items should be folded.

## Shoes

Unless you only own 4 pairs of shoes, you'll need an organization system for them. Without a clear place to put them, shoes can easily pile up on your closet floor or near your front door.

Options to organize your shoes include free-standing shoe racks, under bed shoe organizers, shoe racks that hang on the closet door, or individualized shoe cubes that can stack and sit on your closet shelf. You can also combine different options if needed. Consider how many shoes you need to store and what kind of space you have.

## Accessories

Accessories in your bedroom may include jewelry, purses, belts, ties, hats, or scarves.If you have a closet with space for these items, they'll be stored here. If not, you can also use areas in or near the dresser. For many of these items, some strategically placed hooks can do the trick.

Hats, purses, belts, and scarves can all be stored on simple command hooks hung on the wall inside your closet or a wall in your bedroom. Hats and purses can also be stored on shelves or in bins/baskets as long as nothing heavy is placed on top of them. Scarves and ties can also be placed in bins. Ties can be rolled to fit in smaller spaces or hung on a tie rack. How you store jewelry depends on the kind of jewelry and how much of it you have. Long necklaces can also be hung on small hooks, while other jewelry does best in jewelry boxes or organizers, which come in all shapes and sizes to fit your needs.

## Dressers

If you have a dresser you'll want to be strategic and consistent with where you store items. Ideally, the top drawer holds smaller items such as underwear, socks, or jewelry if it didn't get placed in a jewelry organizer in the closet. To help keep smaller items spaced from one another, use drawer inserts to keep items separated.

Heavier items go toward the bottom of the dresser. These include sweatshirts, sweatpants, jeans, etc. In the middle, you can place pajamas, t-shirts, or other lightweight clothing items that don't need to be folded. Consistency is key when you decide what will go in each drawer so that they don't become a mess.

## Night Tables

Try to keep your night table clear. This is where you might just have a lamp to read at night, you might store a book you are reading or your Kindle in the bedside drawer. Others keep nighttime medications in this area so they don't forget to take them. Always keep medications out of reach if there are children in the home. Essentially your night table is not a major place for storage. Just a few personal items inside and a mostly clear surface aside from maybe a lamp, a photo, or another decorative item.

## Pro Tip for Organizing the Bedroom

Keep in mind that your bedroom should exude peace. This is where you wind down at the end of the day. You really want to keep surfaces clear aside from intentional decor. There's also a good chance that you are underutilizing available storage space that's in your closet, your dresser, or under your bed. Once you organize everything, look around for areas that you can see becoming highly disorganized quickly again. This means that while everything fits, you may need to add an organizer or move smaller things to an even smaller space to avoid items piling up.

## CHAPTER 10

# The Home Office

Your home office needs to be well organized. This is where you work. You want this space to foster productivity. Many of us have rapidly learned to work at home over the past few years, while others may have been doing it for a while before that. Whether you love it or hate it, if you have a home office, you'll need to make sure it is well organized so that you can work efficiently and feel well-prepared when you jump on calls or need to produce something quickly for a client or colleague.

Most home offices have similar components:

- Computer
- Printer
- Books and Files
- Office supplies

## Computer

Considering most things have gone digital, it's possible that your home office space is nothing more than a desk, chair, and computer. Many find that they no longer have a need for anything paper related, while others still need to print and store things.

While a thorough explanation of digital organization is outside the scope of this book, you'll generally approach it with some of the same concepts you have already learned. Keep your desktop from becoming too cluttered with random shortcuts. Your desktop should have just the shortcuts that you'll need. Keep shortcuts with related functions near each other. Create files to categorize items so that they can easily be found later. Use files or labels in your email folder to categorize your emails. Consider adding filters in the settings so that specific emails automatically go under the correct label, rather than piling into the general inbox.

Regarding your actual desk space, it's important to keep the space around your computer clear and ready to work. Having a lot of things around you, like papers and post-its can be distracting. It can also be unpleasant to work in a space that feels overly cluttered. Additionally, keep your cords neat and out of the way.

## Printer

This should be on or near your desk area so that you're not having to walk to another area of the office or to another room to get what you printed. Additionally, keep things like extra paper and ink stored nearby.

## Books and Files

These can be pretty straightforward. Books should be stored on the bookshelf. If you don't have one and you only have a few books in your office, you can use bookends and put them on any nearby shelf or on one end of your desk, depending on the size of your desk space.

Files would be considered any paper that you need or want to keep. To avoid these piling up on your desk, either use a paper organizer that goes on top of the desk with labels to categorize the papers or use a filing drawer with hanging file folders that you can label and store papers that way.

## Office Supplies

These include pens, highlighters, post-its, extra notepads, paperclips, etc. Have one drawer where you can store extra office supplies. Use smaller containers that can sit in that drawer to keep things separated and organized. This way, when you need something, you know exactly where to look.

## Pro Tip for the Home Office

Each time you leave your desk for the day, make sure these items are back where you initially arranged them. It's easy to get disorganized when you are busy working. But your workspace should never feel cluttered or difficult to navigate. You want to look forward to being productive and efficient in your space.

Make your home office space enjoyable to be in. This will also help your productivity. Intentionally choose lighting that you enjoy working in, have a smart speaker so that you can play music while you work, and decorate in a way that inspires you. These things will help you want to maintain the organization and keep this space being one you want to come back to again and again.

# CHAPTER 11

# Laundry and the Laundry Room

Now you might have a separate laundry room, or you might have a smaller living space that doesn't include this room. But either way, we know you have laundry. So let's consider the various aspects that go along with your laundry and how you can keep it all organized.

- Dirty laundry
- Laundry soaps, dryer sheets, fabric softeners, etc.
- Clean laundry

## Dirty Laundry

If you sort your clothes before washing them, have a 3-section laundry sorter so that dirty clothes get immediately sorted after taking them off. Label the sections for your darks, whites, and colors. Keep this sorter in your bedroom because that's where you're most likely to use it. If you put it in the laundry room, chances are your laundry goes on the floor rather than you getting undressed and walking it over the laundry room. You want your system to cater to the path of least resistance.

## Laundry Soap, Dryer Sheets, Fabric Softeners, etc.

Having a wall rack, a small laundry cart, bins, or baskets to hold the supplies that you'll need to do your laundry is essential. These things should be quick and easy to find and always located closest to where they will be used. If you are using bins or baskets, don't forget to label them.

## Clean Laundry

Keeping a drying rack in your laundry room is ideal for the clothes that you don't want to put in the dryer. You can find free-standing or wall-mounted foldable drying racks to keep in your laundry room without taking up too much space.

It's also a good idea to have a small basket near the dryer for unmatched socks. They usually have a way of turning up, and you want one designated spot for them until you find their match. You'll also want a small trash bin for lint after clothes come out of the dryer.

Ideally, you'll be folding your laundry as soon as you pull it out of the dryer, but if we're being realistic, that may not happen every time. This is where a clean laundry basket comes in. If it's one of those times when you are in a rush, or you are in the middle of doing something else, and you had to pull the clothes out of the dryer to start another load, but you don't have the time or patience to fold it all right now, you can put it in a basket in your bedroom designated just for clean clothes. Establish a routine for how frequently you clear this basket. This stops the clean laundry pileup from happening in other places like your bed, a chair, or your couch.

## Pro Tip for the Laundry Room

Depending on the setup of your home, the laundry room can also be a great area to store additional cleaning supplies such as the mop, swiffer, vacuum, etc.

# CHAPTER 12
# Storage and Hallways

Hallways should remain clear aside from any hallway closets or built-in shelving. Shelves that are in the halls should hold minimal decor or deep baskets that give a clean and uniform look to the space.

If the shelves are near an entryway, you can keep things that would be useful when leaving the house, such as a small umbrella, gloves, hat, or sunscreen. If you have built-in shelves instead of a linen closet, these baskets are where you might store extra blankets. These shelves could also be used for books.

Generally, the closet nearest to the entryway is used as the coat closet to hold any coats, rain jackets, umbrellas, hats, gloves, boots, etc. While the closet in the middle of the hallway is often used as a linen closet where you might store extra sheets, towels, blankets, tablecloths, etc. Additional storage closets can keep extra things like cleaning supplies, holiday decorations, and other seasonal items that don't really make sense in any particular room of the house.

## Pro Tip for your Storage

You can often create additional storage space in almost any room. Whether you do this by finding bins that fit under the bed, hanging hooks on the wall of the closet, installing floating shelves in your laundry room, etc. There are always ways to create more storage space.

When storing items, make sure they are clearly labeled so that you know where to find things and you have a clearly designated spot to put them back. Storage spaces can easily get cluttered and disorganized, so make sure you are intentional about where things go so that anyone looking at that space could find what they are looking for.

# Part 3

## Cleaning Room by Room

# CHAPTER 13

# Your Cleaning System

If you are someone who has ADHD and struggles with clutter and organization, chances are your cleaning routine doesn't come naturally either. But once you have a plan and a system for how to address keeping your home clean, you'll find it easier than you think.

By now, you've really begun to master the application of the skills you need to initiate tasks and to see them through to completion. You've done it in the decluttering phase, and you've done it as you reorganized your home and set up systems to keep it decluttered and organized.

Cleaning is really just an additional step. It's essentially an add-on using the same types of skills that you've already been working on. Once you can start to think of cleaning as just an extension of the skills you've already been successfully using, you can break up the tasks into small, manageable, rewarding pieces, and you can start to create a routine that is both structured and flexible enough to keep working for you.

## How Often Should You Clean

How often and in what ways you use a room helps to determine how often you should clean it. Places that get used more often will need to be cleaned more frequently. Places where hygiene is essential, like the bathroom, or where food is involved, like the kitchen, will need a deep cleaning that includes more attention to detail and disinfecting more frequently than, say, the bedroom or laundry room.

Generally, your entire house only needs a solid deep clean 2-3 times yearly. This is the kind of cleaning you see people doing during Spring cleaning where they go through everything, removing extra clutter, dusting and wiping from the ceiling to the floor, and getting behind and under all the furniture.

Daily cleaning is usually pretty simple spot cleaning, general wiping down of areas, and keeping high traffic spots swept. While a weekly or biweekly clean will be more detailed than your daily cleaning including mopping and getting into smaller areas that you might not pay attention to every day. The kitchen, for example, gets a general simple cleaning daily and a more thorough cleaning at least every 1-2 wks.

## What Supplies You'll Need

- Paper towels or reusable clean rags
- Broom
- Mop
- Vacuum
- Multi Surface cleaner
- Disinfectant spray
- White vinegar

- Spray bottles
- Microfiber cloth
- Microfiber mop or duster to reach high places
- Daily shower spray
- Squeegee
- Cleaning caddy

## Make a White Vinegar Cleaning Solution

If you pour white vinegar and water into a spray bottle in a 1:1 ratio, you have a cleaning solution that breaks down dirt and buildup, kills most mold and mildew, and is safe and non-toxic. This can be used when cleaning many areas of your home. The smell of the vinegar should dissipate shortly after you're done cleaning.

# The Secret to Never Getting Overwhelmed by Cleaning Again

We know that part of the reason it is difficult to get organized and clean and maintain it is that the idea of cleaning your whole house can feel daunting. Executive function deficits make it hard to conceptualize what seems to be a very big task with way too many smaller parts. It becomes difficult to identify what to prioritize, where to start, and how to proceed through all of the necessary steps effectively. So, cleaning can become something we might avoid altogether or only do when we absolutely have to.

There are approaches to cleaning that are meant to make it more focused and approachable. There are also an unlimited number of cleaning schedules that have been published that are really meant to make it as simple as print and checking it off the list. You can even use the Daily Weekly Organizer found at this end book.

Take advantage of the visual aids where possible, either by creating your own or using one that is pre-made for you. Using a visual list for your cleaning needs addresses working memory deficits and means that you won't have to rely on remembering what you need to do next or having to break down the components of thoroughly cleaning your kitchen every time. You'll simply follow the list. Some of these lists can be more ADHD-friendly because you don't always have to do the same task every Monday. Instead, if you have tasks that get completed on a weekly basis, then you make sure that each day, you are checking something off that weekly list. It can be whichever task you would prefer to do that day, but something gets checked off.

Next, we'll explore three different approaches to regularly cleaning your home. These are Zone Cleaning, Task Cleaning, and using a Daily/Weekly/Monthly Checklist. As you consider these approaches, take into account your individual needs and the barriers to cleaning that you have experienced up to now. You'll want to focus on choosing the method that is most likely to overcome your individual challenges with cleaning to make the process as easy as possible.

## What is Zone Cleaning?

If you've explored different ways of cleaning your house before, you may have encountered the concept of zone cleaning. It's meant to be an effective method of cleaning that's meant to minimize feelings of anxiety and overwhelm. The idea is that you divide your home into about 5 zones. Those zones may include more than one room grouped together. For example:

Zone 1: Living Room
Zone 2: Kitchen
Zone 3: Bedroom and Home Office
Zone 4: Bathroom
Zone 5: Laundry and Storage

Once you've divided your home into zones, you list deep cleaning tasks for that zone. One of the benefits of zone cleaning is also considered to be that deep cleaning is occurring all year round, so you do not have to plan to do it at any particular point, such as Spring cleaning.

Examples of tasks for Zone 1 Living Room might be:

- Clean the windows
- Dust the ceiling fan
- Vacuum the rugs
- Wash the throw blankets

While tasks for Zone 4 Bathroom might include:

- Scrub the floor
- Clean the toilet
- Wash the bathmats and towels
- Deep clean the shower

Once you've made this list, you commit to doing tasks in that zone for 15 minutes. This may mean only working on one task, or you may get to more than one. Each week, you are only focusing on 1 zone, and each day you are only doing 15 minutes worth of tasks in that zone. There are many free templates of zone cleaning examples available online, or it may make the most sense to make your own so that it's tailored to your home and the tasks you need to accomplish.

## What is Task Cleaning?

Task cleaning differs from zone cleaning by focusing on one particular type of task and applying that throughout the entire house rather than staying in one particular room or zone. The idea is that you may be less likely to become distracted or sidetracked in tidying up other things if you are focused on one particular type of task.

Examples of task cleaning might be:

- Wipe down and disinfect all hard surfaces (tables/countertops)
- Vacuum all carpets/rugs
- Sweep all hard floors
- Dust (remember to go from top to bottom)

You would list all the tasks involved with cleaning your home, choose one task each day, and move through the house completing that task.

## Making a Daily/Weekly/Monthly Checklist

If the above strategies don't feel like they do enough to accomplish the cleaning needs of your home, you might want to consider the Definitive Cleaning Schedule created by Good Housekeeping (Smith & Picard, 2019). They established an ultimate guide for how often cleaning tasks must be completed in your home. With a checklist like this, you could establish your daily routines and then also make sure you are checking something off the list on a weekly and monthly basis.

For example, their daily list includes:

- Clean dirty dishes
- Wipe down kitchen counters and table
- Sweep kitchen floors
- Squeegee shower walls
- Wipe down bathroom surfaces

While their weekly list includes:

- Change bedding
- Clean microwave
- Mop kitchen and bathroom floors
- Scrub bathroom surfaces
- Toss expired food

And things on their monthly list include:

- Dust and clean the light fixtures
- Clean the dishwasher and laundry machines

They suggest tasks that need to be done every 3-6 months, such as:

- Wiping down the inside of your fridge
- Cleaning the shower curtain liner
- Cleaning under and behind furniture
- Cleaning inside the oven

While yearly tasks include:

- Cleaning the drapes and curtains
- Clearing out the gutters
- Deep clean the carpet and upholstery

An extensive checklist like this, with specifically identified timing of when things need to be done, lets you see all of the tasks that need to be done and lets you choose what you'd like to pick from that list. The idea here is that tasks won't be overlooked, but also, you wouldn't need a rigid schedule. As long as you set aside time in your daily/weekly schedule for cleaning, you can choose what goes in those time blocks based on what you prefer to do. You could also change it up on a weekly basis.

## Establishing the Right System for You

Finding the system that works for you means taking into account which ones you are most likely to do. After reading through these options, you might not be sure, and that is okay. You can start with one and see how that works. However, if you know that you are likely to get sidetracked with different tasks in a room, then task cleaning may be a better fit for you. On the other hand, if the idea of doing one task throughout the entire house seems daunting, then zone cleaning may be a better fit because of the more narrow focus on one area for a set amount of time.

Some prefer the checklist option because they can be certain that things in the house are getting done at the pace they should be cleaned. However, they are not stuck to a rigid schedule. As long as they set aside time for cleaning, they can pick and choose based on

145

what's still left on the list. This adds some novelty to the process and allows more flexibility based on what you feel like or don't feel like doing.

When applying any of these systems, you need to make them work for you. Tailor them to your home and your needs. Having a visual plan that you can check off makes you more likely to complete the tasks that need to be done.

Keep in mind that you'll be establishing some habits around your daily cleaning needs, such as making the bed, wiping down counters, and doing dishes. With these habits becoming part of your normal living routine, they wouldn't necessarily have to be scheduled into your cleaning time. For example, making the bed just becomes what you do when you get out of bed. Wiping the counters and table is just what you do after you've prepared or eaten food in the kitchen, etc. Habit stacking, in this way, frees up space in your calendar and in your day to really consider where the other cleaning tasks will go.

# Don't Skip Out on the Details

When going through your cleaning process, it is helpful to have an understanding of some basic details. You'll want to clean in the most efficient way possible so that you're not having to backtrack over work you've already done.

## The Best Order to Clean

Soak First

Where chemicals and cleaning solutions are involved, anything that needs to soak should be done first. This way, you can spray and allow it to soak while you move on to other things in that room. So that after you've accomplished other things, you can come back to easily wipe it down, and you don't waste time simply waiting for it to be ready.

Clean Before Disinfecting

Disinfecting an area first just defeats the purpose. It should be the last stage of cleaning that area. First, wipe it down, clean it, then disinfect it before you are done.

Top Down

Clean from the top down. In other words, you are not going to clean the floor and then wipe down the counters. This means you are potentially wiping crumbs and debris onto your clean floor. In any room you are cleaning, clean high first and make your way down to the floor so that you are not inadvertently doubling your work.

In addition to making sure that the floors are the last thing to be cleaned in a room, make sure that you sweep or vacuum before you mop. Even if it doesn't look like it needs to be swept or vacuumed, the last thing you want to do is to be swirling around dirt and debris while you mop.

## How to Clean without Wasting Time and Energy

Not having a plan, doing things in the wrong order, and doing them incorrectly can waste time. You don't want to put the effort into cleaning and organizing only to have to go back over things you have already done. You also don't want a task that should take 10 minutes to take 30 minutes. Take a look at these common time wasters and how to accomplish your cleaning tasks as efficiently as possible.

Check Your Cleaning Tools

Make sure your cleaning tools themselves are clean. When gathering the items in your caddy or verifying that you have everything you need in there, take a look and make sure that the things you are using aren't just going to spread more dirt and grime around. The brushes, cloths, or sponges you are using should be clean.

It Needs to be Clean Before It Can Shine

Another common mistake is not cleaning surfaces before you expect them to shine. Your mirror is a good example. Often people will apply the glass cleaner, wipe it, and become confused about why it didn't work. Make sure you wipe down the mirror or television set with a clean damp cloth first, then dry, then apply the glass cleaner and wipe.

You probably don't need to scrub

Don't scrub, soak. Anything that requires sufficient scrubbing should be soaked first. Whether this means you spray it thoroughly and let it set for 20 minutes before you try to wipe it down or you soap up a pan and leave it soaking in the sink before you try to wash it. Don't waste time and energy scrubbing when soaking can break down the mess for you. This is where your white vinegar solution can often come in handy. The acidity in the vinegar can break down dirt and grime when left to soak. So spray it, go clean something else, and come back to it.

Don't clean your windows in the sun

Don't clean your windows when the sun is beating on them. Your glass cleaner will dry faster than you can wipe it, leaving you with a streaky finish. Wait for cloudy days, or aim to clean your windows in the morning or evening so that your windows get a nice streak-free shine the first time around.

What are your cleaning cloths made of?

Choosing cleaning cloths that are the wrong material. Nothing is worse than trying to clean and leaving lint or fibers behind as you're cleaning. Go for microfiber cloths in your cleaning caddy. These cloths are more effective at wiping away bacteria, and they can easily be tossed in the laundry.

Clean your vacuum

Empty your vacuum bag or container frequently. Having a full vacuum at best makes it weaker and more time-consuming to pick anything up, but beyond that, some vacuums will start to kick out dust and dirt through the exhaust, making your space even messier than when you started. It's a good idea to empty the bag or container and remove the hair from the brushes after each use so that you're not wasting time the next time you use it.

Clean as you go

Try to clean as you go. Some people make the mistake of saving things for when their cleaning session is scheduled. This is a good way to let a spill set so it takes more time to clean later. Also, you aren't doing future you any favors by adding on to the task and potentially making it more overwhelming than it needed to be. If something spills try to normalize wiping it up right then and there. If you prepare food, get used to wiping down the counters immediately. Spraying and squeegeeing the shower after each use will make your shower deep cleaning a lot easier and less time consuming.

## Schedule Your Cleaning in Advance

Just like many other aspects of your decluttering and organizing systems, you have to make time for cleaning rather than waiting for time to be available. While you'll want to make certain aspects of your cleaning system become part of your daily habits, such as wiping down the table after you've eaten a meal, you still want to use your calendar or planner to set aside 15-30 minutes daily to accomplish cleaning tasks.

Depending on the cleaning system you create, you might do 30 minutes every weekday and take off on the weekends. Or you might do 15 minutes each day and have an hour set aside over the weekend to do a deeper clean. Whatever schedule you decide to implement, make sure that it's in your planner so that you see it, you have a reminder, and you'll be more likely to follow through.

Additionally, have a clear cleaning plan. Executive dysfunction makes it really inefficient to approach a room and start figuring out how to clean it right then and there. It's more likely that you'll spend a lot more time figuring things out and accomplishing less than you would have if you had a clear plan to follow. Have it written out so that all you need to do is look at the list, do what it says, and check it off. This takes the cognitive effort out of the equation and makes the task itself more tangible.

## Don't be afraid to ask for help

If you live with a roommate, partner, or other family members, ask them to help out in the process. Enlisting help can be more motivating, it can help keep you accountable and it can get the job done!

If you live alone, you can still get help from your friends or family. If it's a big cleaning job, you might ask them to come over to help you get it done. This applies to things like Spring cleaning, or cleaning for the first time in a while. Another way of getting help from friends and family includes body doubling. If you have a friend who has also wanted to get their own cleaning system on track, you can motivate each other by cleaning together on a video call. This helps keep you accountable, it is more motivating to do the activity while you see someone else also doing it, and the reward here is social. You and your friend have a shared goal of getting your cleaning on track and you are both working on it together.

Even if you are not sure whether your friends or family will want to come over to help or body double with you on the phone, it doesn't hurt to ask. The worst thing they can do is say no, and then you haven't really lost anything.

## Managing Boring Tasks & How to make cleaning more fun

As we've discussed in depth, if the task is boring, people with ADHD are much less likely to start or follow through with it. You'll need to find ways to make it less boring and a bit more fun. Take into account your preference for immediate gratification, your reward system, and your impulsivity which drives you toward more spontaneity rather than rigid schedules. These can all be leveraged if you are intentional about how you proceed with your cleaning system.

## Make it Rewarding

Find something you genuinely enjoy or are interested in and pair it with your cleaning tasks. Listening to podcasts or TED talks, audiobooks, upbeat music playlists, or talking with a friend on the phone. These are all ways to make your cleaning tasks more enjoyable and rewarding because you are incorporating something that you are interested in, that you like to do, or that makes you feel good. These things will also have your mind occupied more with the fun thing while your hands do the cleaning. Time will pass more quickly this way and you won't be focused on thinking about how boring or unenjoyable the task itself is.

## Be Spontaneous

Yes, you'll need to schedule time for cleaning. However, you have some wiggle room when it comes to exactly what you do during that cleaning time. Whether you opt for zone cleaning, task-based cleaning, or cleaning according to your daily/weekly/monthly checklist, none of these approaches requires that you do the same thing every Monday at 10am.

The benefit of each of these approaches is in the combination of structure and flexibility that they allow. There is enough structure to ensure that things that need to be cleaned are not being neglected and falling through the cracks. But there is also enough wiggle room to say that if you don't feel like vacuuming right now, you can probably just as easily choose something else on the list. Unless you've done everything else and in that case, yes, it is time to vacuum.

The ability to choose which things you want to do and when also gives you more of a sense of control over the whole cleaning system.

So, rather than feeling like this is something that you are stuck doing, this is something that you own and can shape in the way that best suits you and your household.

Now that you've got a good sense of what you'll need and how your cleaning system can work, you can start to establish clear plans for each room in your house. As a foundation, you can start with the information here, and adapt it to what works for you.

# CHAPTER 14

# How to Clean Each Room

The following sections will take you through the rationale for how to approach each room, the supplies you'll need, and how frequently each task should be done. As with other sections of this book, these things can be adapted to fit your needs. Your frequency of cleaning may be different if for example, you have pets, or if you travel for work and spend several days each week away from home. These are meant to give you a general starting point as you establish your own cleaning routine.

## The Living Room

The living room is the main hub of your house. This is where you'll spend time relaxing and also the first place your guests will see and where they will spend the most time. This makes your living room a priority in the cleaning system that you create, but luckily if you don't spend much time eating in your living room and if you address any spills as they occur, this room is not one that requires frequent heavy-duty cleaning.

## Supplies

Things you may need when cleaning the living room include:

- A duster
- White vinegar solution
- Window cleaner
- A few microfiber cloths
- A vacuum
- A mop and bucket
- Furniture polish

Depending on the approach you have decided on for cleaning, you may not need all of these items at once, however, it is useful to know which supplies will generally be used in this room.

Assuming you've been staying on top of the clutter and you've been maintaining your organization system, you are ready to clean up! If things have slid back a bit, make sure that you tidy up before you start cleaning.

## Daily

- General upkeep, wiping up spills

## Weekly

- Dust
- Wipe down surfaces
- Vacuum or Sweep and Mop
  - This may be more frequent with children or pets

## Monthly

- Clean the windows, wipe down window frames
- Clean mirrors
- Polishing furniture and cleaning upholstery if needed

# The Bathroom

The bathroom is a high-traffic area that has the potential to get dirty quickly. Luckily it tends to be a smaller room, but this room has more daily and weekly cleaning needs than you saw in the living room.

## Supplies

It's generally a good idea to keep these cleaning items stored in your bathroom if you have the space.

- Multi-surface bathroom cleaner
- Daily shower spray
- Glass cleaner
- Toilet bowl cleaner
- Disinfecting wipes
- Toilet brush
- Spray bottle
- Handheld squeegee
- Sponges or microfiber clothes

## Daily

- Spray and squeegee the shower
- Wipe down the sink, counter, and other surfaces
- Change hand towels, especially if being used by multiple people

## Weekly

- Wash all the towels and bathmats
- Clean and disinfect the toilet
- Mop the bathroom floors
- Cleaning the shower and tub
- Wipe down the mirrors and cabinets
- Empty the trash

## Monthly

- Clean the shower curtain
- Clean windows

# The Kitchen

The kitchen is another high-traffic area that is likely one of the central hubs in your home for both you and your guests. Because you are preparing and cooking food, likely making some daily messes, doing dishes, and cleaning the sink area regularly, this would be considered more of a high-priority area in your cleaning system.

## Supplies

- Disinfectant wipes, spray, and floor cleaner
- White vinegar solution, spray bottle
- Rubber gloves
- Microfiber cloths
- Mop, bucket
- Multi-purpose cleaner

- Oven cleaner
- Stainless steel cleaner (if your appliances are stainless)
- Scrubbing sponges
- Dish soap

## Daily

- Do the dishes
- Sweep the floor
- Clean up spills as they occur
- Wipe down the sink, countertops, range top, and kitchen table top

## Weekly

- Mop the floors
- Wipe down cabinets
- Wipe down the appliances
- Change the dishtowels
- Go through the fridge to toss any old leftovers

## Monthly

- Clean the oven
- Wipe down and spray the refrigerator shelves to clean and disinfect
- Clean the inside of the microwave with the white vinegar solution
- Clean your coffee maker - running white vinegar mixed with water through to descale it

- Wipe down the outside and inside of the cabinets
  - Pull out the food, pull out the shelf liners and clean them, wiping down anything that may have spilled

# The Bedroom

Out of all the spaces in the house, this one should be your sanctuary. As such it should be clean so that you can feel comfortable and relaxed. Although you spend time in your bedroom daily, this wouldn't be considered a high-traffic area, the cleaning needs are not too intense here.

## Supplies

- Microfiber cloths
- Vacuum / Mop and bucket
- White vinegar solution
- Multipurpose cleaner
- Glass cleaner

## Daily

- Daily cleaning here is more associated with decluttering and organizing
  - Making your bed
  - Tidying up any clutter
  - Clean and Dirty laundry are in the right place
  - Weekly
- Change your sheets and pillowcases
- Dust your furniture
- Mop or vacuum the floor

## Monthly

- Wash comforters
- Wipe down walls and baseboards
- Clean light fixtures
- Shake out any area rugs
- Clean the mirrors and windows
- Dust the ceiling fans, vents, and air conditioning units

# The Home Office

The home office is an area that you'll use almost every day, but luckily cleaning it is typically pretty simple. Here are the things you'll need to keep it clean:

## Supplies

- Microfiber cloth
- Duster
- Multi-purpose spray cleaner
- Disinfectant spray or wipes
- Glass cleaner
- Vacuum
- mop/bucket

## Daily

- Wipe down your workspace

## Weekly

- Dust
- Vacuum/mop
- Disinfect keyboard and mouse

## Monthly

- Clean windows

# Laundry and the Laundry Room

While it is normal to do about one load of laundry per week, exactly how often you do loads of wash can differ based on several factors:

- How many times you change clothes, including:
  - Gym clothes
  - Work uniforms
  - Getting dressed for evening social events
- How many people are in your household
- Whether you do your laundry at home or at the laundromat

All of the above factors will influence your approach to doing the laundry. Generally, you don't want to have to do more than one or two loads to get all of your laundry done. This may mean you do laundry 2-3 times per week, depending on how many clothes you are going through. Otherwise, the task can feel too daunting to complete. However, if you go to the laundromat, then a weekly routine might make more sense - even if that means 4 loads since you can use multiple machines at once.

If you do your laundry in your own home, you may choose to split up when you wash and dry. For example, you might start a load right before you leave for work in the morning, and you might put it in the dryer as soon as you get home from work. Generally, clothing can be left in the washer for up to 8-12 hours without building up any mildew or getting that musty smell. Often laundry can feel daunting because we know a full wash and dry cycle takes about 2 hours. That can feel like a large block of time to set aside. Breaking it up might help you do it more frequently instead of procrastinating until you have no pants left.

If you've left a load of clothes in the dryer for too long, you don't need to run an entire dry cycle or pull out the iron to get the wrinkles out. Simply take a damp hand towel and toss it in with your dry clothes. Then run the dryer for 10 minutes. This should de-wrinkle them so that you can fold them without having to waste more time.

Your clothes will be cleaned more effectively if you do smaller loads. You want your clothes to move around freely in the soap and water versus being tightly packed in and immobile, so that they can actually get clean. Additionally, try to wash similar clothes together. If you have a laundry organizer that allows you to separate your laundry as soon as you put it in the hamper, that makes it easier. Similar colors and materials will have similar washing instructions. Following the instructions on the tag will keep your clothes in the best shape for longer. For example, dark clothes will keep their color longer when washed in cold water.

As for the laundry room itself, this area has a tendency to get dusty. With all of the fabric, dirt, debris, and lint involved, you'll be sweeping and wiping down this area regularly to keep it looking clean. Otherwise, your laundry room upkeep tends to be pretty easy.

## Supplies

- Multipurpose cleaner
- Microfiber cloths
- broom/mop/bucket
- Glass cleaner
- White vinegar

## Daily

- Sweep
- Clean up any soap spills
- Empty lint trap in the dryer

## Weekly

- Mop the floors
- Wipe down the machines
- Dust/wipe down any other surfaces

## Monthly

- Clean the windows
- Wipe down the baseboards and walls to prevent any dust buildup
- Run an empty wash cycle with white vinegar to clean your washing machine

## Storage and Hallways

Hallways throughout the house will differ in the amount of traffic they get. Storage areas typically won't get much traffic and will really only require monthly maintenance if they're not used frequently.

### Supplies

- broom/mop/bucket or vacuum
- White vinegar solution or another floor cleaner
- Microfiber cloths
- duster

### Daily

- Sweep high traffic areas

### Weekly

- Dust any light fixtures, shelves, or decor in the halls
- Sweep and mop or vacuum

### Monthly

- Wipe down the walls and baseboards
- Dust and wipe down surfaces in your storage areas
- Depending on the storage area, vacuum or sweep and mop the floor

As you consider the things that need to be done daily, weekly, and monthly, you can figure out where you would like them to go in your regular cleaning schedule. Whether you opt for zone cleaning, task-based cleaning, or simply choosing from the checklist based on how frequently things need to get done and fitting the tasks into your time blocks, cleaning should now feel more tangible.

Cleaning can feel overwhelming when we consider all of the tasks that go into maintaining a clean home, but not everything gets done every day, and when you break it down in ways that work for you, your schedule, and your household, you'll find that it's a lot easier to maintain a clean and organized home than you initially thought.

# Conclusion

By now, you have a better understanding of how ADHD impacts you and how you can leverage the characteristics that are common to ADHD to overcome your challenges and accomplish your goals. Cleaning and organizing become tangible when we break them down and structure them in a way that works for us.

Establishing habits and systems are the key to maintaining a clean and organized home in the long term. The reason it has not worked for you before, is that much of the advice out there is not specific to people with ADHD.

Bear in mind that it is normal for people with ADHD to fall out of a routine. That's okay, and self compassion goes much further than beating yourself up. You have the skills, and once you've created a habit and a system, it's much easier to start again. Keeping this manual as your guide and adapting the skills to suit your preferences and needs, I'm confident you'll be able to master the ability to maintain a neat and organized home that helps you function better and that you can be proud of.

# Sample Calendar

Check out the schedule below for an idea of what your decluttering, organizing, and cleaning systems might look like in your monthly calendar. You'll notice that this maintenance system really doesn't require much time each day. It's more about consistency and staying on track with the tasks that need to get done. Remember that this is just one example and the maintenance system you set up for yourself may be different depending on your needs and your lifestyle.

## May 2023

**Daily:** Bathroom - spray/squeegee/wipe shower & sink after shower
Kitchen: Wipe surfaces, sweep after dinner
Declutter x10 min 730am & 530pm; Organize x15min 545pm

| Monday | Tuesday | Wednesday | Thursday | Friday | Saturday | Sunday |
|---|---|---|---|---|---|---|
| 1<br>6pm<br>Paperwork<br>x15min | 2<br>6pm<br>Clean Toilet &<br>Shower<br>(30min) | 3<br>6pm<br>Empty Trash | 4<br>Do Laundry<br>8am Wash<br>5pm Dry | 5<br>530pm<br>Re-Organize<br>x30min<br>Fold Clothes | 6<br>Vacuum / Mop<br>Floors | 7<br>Clean<br>Windows &<br>Mirrors |
| 8<br>6pm<br>Paperwork<br>x15min | 9<br>6pm<br>Clean Toilet &<br>Shower<br>(30min) | 10<br>6pm<br>Empty Trash | 11<br>Do Laundry<br>8am Wash<br>5pm Dry | 12<br>530pm<br>Re-Organize<br>x30min<br>Fold Clothes | 13<br>Vacuum / Mop<br>Floors | 14<br>Clean Shower<br>Curtain |
| 15<br>6pm<br>Paperwork<br>x15min | 16<br>6pm<br>Clean Toilet &<br>Shower<br>(30min) | 17<br>6pm<br>Empty Trash | 18<br>Do Laundry<br>8am Wash<br>5pm Dry | 19<br>530pm<br>Re-Organize<br>x30min<br>Fold Clothes | 20<br>Vacuum / Mop<br>Floors | 21<br>Clean Fridge<br>& Coffee<br>Maker |
| 22<br>6pm<br>Paperwork<br>x15min | 23<br>6pm<br>Clean Toilet &<br>Shower<br>(30min) | 24<br>6pm<br>Empty Trash | 25<br>Do Laundry<br>8am Wash<br>5pm Dry | 26<br>530pm<br>Re-Organize<br>x30min<br>Fold Clothes | 27<br>Vacuum / Mop<br>Floors | 28<br>Clean Fridge<br>& Coffee<br>Maker |
| 29<br>6pm<br>Paperwork<br>x15min | 30<br>6pm<br>Clean Toilet &<br>Shower<br>(30min) | 31<br>6pm<br>Empty Trash | | | | |

# Daily Weekly Organizer

Check out the Daily Weekly Organizer below for an idea of how you can schedule your cleaning systems. Like the monthly calendar above your system might have some differences so it's more tailored to you. Use the Organizer as a template to understand how tasks and rooms can fit into a week and be easy to manage.

Get Your Daily Organizer by using the link if you're reading on an ebook device, or by scanning the QR code below:

# References

American Psychiatric Association. (2013). *Diagnostic and statistical manual of mental disorders* (5th ed.). https://doi.org/10.1176/appi.books.9780890425596

Arnsten A. F. (2015). Stress weakens prefrontal networks: molecular insults to higher cognition. *Nature neuroscience, 18*(10), 1376–1385. https://doi.org/10.1038/nn.4087

Carr-Fanning, K. (2020). Understanding ADHD and its impact. *Irish Medical Times, 54*(10), 28-28,30. http://library.capella.edu/login?qurl=https%3A%2F%2Fwww.proque st.com%2Ftrade-journals%2Funderstanding-adhd-impact%2Fdocview%2F2448683599%2Fse-2%3Faccountid%3D27965 https://chadd.org/for-adults/organizing-the-home-and-office-space/

Clear, James. (2018). Atomic habits: an easy & proven way to build good habits & break bad ones . Penguin: Avery.

Grimm, O., van Rooij, D., Tshagharyan, A., Yildiz, D., Leonards, J., Elgohary, A., Buitelaar, J., & Reif, A. (2021). Effects of comorbid disorders on reward processing and connectivity in adults with ADHD. *Translational psychiatry*, *11*(1), 636. https://doi.org/10.1038/s41398-021-01758-0

Durand, G., Arbone, I. S., & Wharton, M. (2020). Reduced organizational skills in adults with ADHD are due to deficits in persistence, not in strategies. *PeerJ*, *8*, e9844. https://doi.org/10.7717/peerj.9844

Khadka, S., Pearlson, G. D., Calhoun, V. D., Liu, J., Gelernter, J., Bessette, K. L., & Stevens, M. C. (2016). Multivariate Imaging Genetics Study of MRI Gray Matter Volume and SNPs Reveals Biological Pathways Correlated with Brain Structural Differences in Attention Deficit Hyperactivity Disorder. *Frontiers in psychiatry* , *7* , 128. https://doi.org/10.3389/fpsyt.2016.00128

Hvolby A. (2015). Associations of sleep disturbance with ADHD: implications for treatment. *Attention deficit and hyperactivity disorders*, *7*(1), 1–18. https://doi.org/10.1007/s12402-014-0151-0

Lazar, S. W., Kerr, C. E., Wasserman, R. H., Gray, J. R., Greve, D. N., Treadway, M. T., McGarvey, M., Quinn, B. T., Dusek, J. A., Benson, H., Rauch, S. L., Moore, C. I., & Fischl, B. (2005). Meditation experience is associated with increased cortical thickness. *Neuroreport*, *16*(17), 1893–1897. https://doi.org/10.1097/01.wnr.0000186598.66243.19

Lynch, F. A., Moulding, R., & McGillivray, J. A. (2017). Phenomenology of hoarding in children with comorbid attention-deficit/hyperactivity disorder (ADHD): The perceptions of parents. *Comprehensive Psychiatry, 76*, 1-10. https://doi.org/10.1016/j.comppsych.2017.03.009

Mehren, A., Reichert, M., Coghill, D., Müller, H. H. O., Braun, N., & Philipsen, A. (2020). Physical exercise in attention deficit hyperactivity disorder - evidence and implications for the treatment of borderline personality disorder. *Borderline personality disorder and emotion dysregulation, 7*, 1. https://doi.org/10.1186/s40479-019-0115-2

Nall, R., & Klein, A. (2021). *ADHD Benefits: What the Research Says, Creativity & More*. Healthline. Retrieved March 20, 2023, from https://www.healthline.com/health/adhd/benefits-of-adhd#personality-strengths

Sjöwall, D., Roth, L., Lindqvist, S., & Thorell, L. B. (2013). Multiple deficits in ADHD: Executive dysfunction, delay aversion, reaction time variability, and emotional deficits. *Journal of Child Psychology and Psychiatry, 54*(6), 619-627. https://doi.org/10.1111/jcpp.12006

Smith, L., & Picard, C. (2019, March 22). *House Cleaning Schedule - The Cleaning Checklist You Need*. Good Housekeeping. Retrieved April 21, 2023, from https://www.goodhousekeeping.com/home/cleaning/a37462/how-often-you-should-clean-everything/

Society for Neuroscience. (2008, August 21). One Sleepless Night Increases Dopamine In The Human Brain. *ScienceDaily*. Retrieved March 24, 2023 from www.sciencedaily.com/releases/2008/08/080819213033.htm

Steel, P. (2011). The procrastination equation: How to Stop Putting Things Off and Start Getting Stuff Done. New York: Harper.

stress.org/mental-health-apps

Tripp, G., & Wickens, J. R. (2009). Neurobiology of ADHD. *Neuropharmacology*, *57*(7-8), 579–589. https://doi.org/10.1016/j.neuropharm.2009.07.026

Volkow, N. D., Wang, G. J., Kollins, S. H., Wigal, T. L., Newcorn, J. H., Telang, F., Fowler, J. S., Zhu, W., Logan, J., Ma, Y., Pradhan, K., Wong, C., & Swanson, J. M. (2009). Evaluating dopamine reward pathway in ADHD: clinical implications. *JAMA* , *302* (10), 1084–1091. https://doi.org/10.1001/jama.2009.1308

Weissenberger, S., Schonova, K., Büttiker, P., Fazio, R., Vnukova, M., Stefano, G. B., & Ptacek, R. (2021). Time Perception is a Focal Symptom of Attention-Deficit/Hyperactivity Disorder in Adults. *Medical science monitor : international medical journal of experimental and clinical research*, *27*, e933766. https://doi.org/10.12659/MSM.933766

Zhao, S., & Toichi, M. (2020). The Effect of Music Intervention on Attention in Children: Experimental Evidence. *Frontiers in Neuroscience*, *14*. https://doi.org/10.3389/fnins.2020.00757

Zheng, Q., Wang, X., Chiu, K. Y., & Shum, K. K. (2022). Time Perception Deficits in Children and Adolescents with ADHD: A Meta-analysis. *Journal of Attention Disorders*, *26*(2), 267–281. https://doi.org/10.1177/1087054720978557

# THANK YOU

I appreciate you purchasing this book and taking the time to read it. I sincerely hope it has been valuable for you, and that the information inside it has made a positive different in your life.

Before you leave, I'd like to ask you a small favor. Can you please consider reviewing this book on the platform? Leaving a review is an easy and incredibly effective way to support inde- pendent authors like me, so we can keep working.

Hearing your feedback helps me write books that can make an even bigger difference in your life, and the lives of every reader. I would deeply appreciate hearing what you have to say. Click the link below, or scan the QR code to leave a review.

Printed in Great Britain
by Amazon

55706124R00101